D1454008

GOUDY'S TYPE DESIGNS:
HIS STORY AND SPECIMENS

Frederic W. Goudy at his pantograph. Photograph by Earl
Emmons, from the Rochester Institute of Technology
Collection and reproduced with permission, through the
courtesy of Professor Alexander S. Lawson. The "flower"
on the title page (and the cover of the paperback edition) is
a logotype designed by Goudy, taken from his book, *The
Alphabet*, 1918.

GOUDY'S
Type Designs

HIS STORY AND SPECIMENS

Being a virtual facsimile of The Typophiles
Chap Books XIII and XIV
A Half-Century of Type Design and Typography

BY

FREDERIC W. GOUDY

L.H.D. LITT.D. LL.D.

Edited by Paul A. Bennett
with an Introduction by J. Ben Lieberman
and a Bibliography by George J. McKay

SECOND EDITION

New Rochelle, New York: The Myriade Press
1978

© 1946 by Paul A. Bennett for the Typophiles
© 1973 by The Typophiles, Inc.
As Typophiles Chap Books XIII and XIV
*A Half-Century of Type Design and
Typography, 1895-1945*

Second Edition
by arrangement with The Typophiles
through the courtesy of Dr. Robert L. Leslie

Book II, The Treasures of Typography Series ™
© 1978, The Myriade Press
Seven Stony Run, New Rochelle, N.Y. 10804
Printed in the United States of America
All rights reserved.

Library of Congress Number: 77-014886

ISBN: Trade: 0-918142-05-9
Paper: 0-918142-04-0

PUBLISHER'S NOTE

This book—which is not only Goudy's autobiography but certainly the most complete record to date of a typographic contribution that has had major worldwide and permanent effect—was published in 1946 as Typophiles Chap Books XIII and XIV, titled *A Half-Century of Type Design and Typography, 1895-1945*, in 725 copies only, and never reissued. We are proud and pleased to be able to make this virtual facsimile available to a much wider readership.

So that it can be a working tool for students and professionals alike, as well as a Treasure of Typography Book, this edition is not an exact copy. Changes were made, primarily in arrangement, to make it a more convenient reference and to keep its price as low as possible. These changes are described in detail on Page 285. And we have taken the liberty of retitling the book, to make it more explicit and thus more recognizable in its deserved role of a printing classic.

No material in the first edition has been omitted, and by and large the temptation has been resisted to expand or update the book. This is, after all, Goudy's own story, as he saw it. The three exceptions are (1) an introduction by Dr. J. Ben Lieberman, who was chairman of the International Goudy Centennial Committee in 1965-66 and founder of the Goudy Society, (2) the addition of the full alphabet of Goudy Thirty, because he obviously wished he could include it in the first edition but was constrained by the very conception of the typeface as a posthumous statement, and (3) a footnote updating the name change of the Californian face, to make the book a complete record of Goudy's faces.

This edition has been printed offset, of course, instead of letterpress as in the first Typophiles edition. Great care was taken in photographing a copy of the original books and printing with minimal distortion, to present Goudy's typefaces as faithfully as possible.

THE CONTENTS

INTRODUCTION: THE LIVING GOUDY

Frederic W. Goudy, as was noted in the program for the banquet ending his centennial year (1965-66), "was a genius and a giant among type designers, and he ranks with the other immortals who altered fundamentally the styles of our typefaces."

However, for almost two decades before that was written, after Goudy's death in 1947, he had gone almost completely out of fashion, and arbiters of typographic taste sneered at his name and typefaces. Even such a close supporter as Paul A. Bennett (who edited this book) was highly dubious that a Goudy Centennial could succeed. For practical purposes, Goudy was *really* dead.

And then a miracle occurred during the centennial. Goudy arose from the grave that had been dug for him, for at least three reasons:

First, perspective showed that Goudy's truly popular typefaces and his practical example to type manufacturers helped lift American printing (and thus in the long run all Western printing) to a much higher general, *public* level of aesthetic excellence than could have been expected from the second printing revolution (i.e., when, at the turn of the century, mechanical typecasting took over from a basically hand technology).

Second, art and type directors who had been taught to disdain Goudy sight unseen finally opened their eyes to look for themselves, and discovered that Goudy had as many as a dozen faces that might each give him immortality; no past designer's immortality rested on more than one.

Third, Goudy was recognized as a convincing symbol for discerning designers and printers who were worrying about the *third* printing revolution just then getting into full swing: high-technology, computerized typesetting, with the same threat as before, that machinery would snuff out the spirit—the human control—of printing. Here was a man, a very warm and human person, who had joyfully embraced the machine instead of resisting it, as most printing aesthetes had done; he had most successfully merged classic forms and beauty with modern functions, needs and tastes. He had shown that the human being *can* control the machine. A new generation is taking hope because of Goudy's example.

You will have to read between the lines of Goudy's homespun account of his work, in this book, to appreciate what has just been said. It will take awareness, too, to realize Goudy was really creating a new style of typeface that *did* make him an immortal—unrecognized because unlike the styles of Garamond and Bodoni and the others, his did not have specific earmarks. It was a qualitative difference, his creation of the *personal* style of typeface, by which the designer defines the nuances of his own sense of beautiful letterforms and fits them into the modes of his day and the unobtrusiveness required by silent reading. Hermann Zapf is the great example of the personal style in our generation.

But the personal style courts oblivion for a given face. Each one is designed for its own time, and times change. As with paintings, however, some are of such "right" form that they live on as classics. And Goudy, to repeat, produced as many as a dozen which are such works of art: Californian, Deepdene, Garamont, Goudy Cursive, Goudy Mediaeval, Goudy Modern, Goudy Old Style, Goudy Text, Goudy Thirty, Kennerley, Italian Old Style and Village No. 2, not to mention other more specialized faces

8

such as Cloister Initials, Copperplate Gothic, Forum, Friar, Hadriano, Pabst and Ornate that may join our permanent working Typorama (i.e., the full palette or range of faces available for designers and printers) once electronic composition shakes itself out and begins to polarize around known designers instead of scattering widely.

Fred Goudy, health and eyesight failing over his last few years, did not complete any faces beyond those recorded in this book.

Those of you who know Goudy's type thus will have, in this long-out-of-print book, the most complete collection of his faces, one of the world's true treasures. The newcomer to Goudy will have in addition, if he looks with open eyes, the joy of discovering that great treasure.

—*J. Ben Lieberman*

A
HALF-CENTURY OF
Type Design
AND TYPOGRAPHY
1895-1945

BY

FREDERIC W. GOUDY

L.H.D. LITT.D. LL.D.

VOLUME ONE

NEW YORK · THE TYPOPHILES

MCMXLVI

[Title page of the original edition]

PROLOGUE

THE writing of these simple annals of a craftsman has been in the main a labor of love. I cannot refrain from expressing a degree of pride in the accomplishment of such a considerable volume of work as is here presented, and my conscience fears neither the accusing fingers of the ghosts of past designers nor an accusation of plagiarism by the living.

In writing the book I have had two purposes in mind, neither of which is an egotistical desire to exploit my own work, nor indeed to set down here anything more than the plain, simple facts of my work as a type designer. My first purpose is to fix unmistakably the paternity of the types themselves, since several of my designs have already been credited in error to others; and my second is to tell something of the personal reasons leading to the designing of them, facts that could not be known so completely to any biographer as to myself.

I am under no illusions as to what I have attempted to do, and while possibly some of my types may now seem a waste of time and effort and material, at the time of their creation they presented problems I wished to solve. No one attains the mountain peak by a single leap, but rather step by step: my type work has been just as simple as that; one design, then another, always striving, always hoping that each new essay would better the designs which preceded it.

As a traditionalist I have taken the essence (as I saw it) of the early craftsmen's work to intensify my own handicraft; but I insist that I have not allowed myself to be "enslaved by the work of bygone days," nor have I attempted to impose on my own productions the superficialities of the past. "I have never marched in the wake of the latest movements in type design, nor have I been seduced into following the slimy trail of 'art nouveau'." I passed every design I made through the refining fire of study and research, and trusted that the result might bear the stamp of reason. The vagaries of the faddist have never had even a casual interest for me. I have endeavored always to produce thoughtful, dignified type faces of legibility with a degree of distinction and beauty, "freshly risen from the canons of good type design"; attempting to secure in them the negative quality of unpretentiousness and avoiding any fantastic exhibition of self-conscious preciosity.

With little erudition and even less literary skill, I have tried to present my story in an interesting manner, although I fear it can have little interest save to the few who care for type, typography, craftsmanship, and the like. I have plans for more work—to stop now would probably mean the end of life itself. I ask only that it may be said of me too, as it was said of William Morris, that "he sought to do good work within the limits of his own craft."

Frederic W. Goudy

Deepdene
Marlboro-on-Hudson, New York
October 5, 1944

ACKNOWLEDGMENTS

THE author thanks Paul A. Bennett for his painstaking help in the preparation of the text and many helpful suggestions in the making of this Chap Book; Peter Beilenson for seeing the book through the press; and the Lanston Monotype Machine Company for furnishing specimens of the types designed for the Company and some of the types reproduced by it under a royalty agreement with the author. He wishes also to thank the American Typefounders Company for furnishing specimens of the types designed by the author which the Company produced. He thanks also Howard Coggeshall and many other printer friends, who own those types of which the matrices were destroyed by the Village Foundry fire, for furnishing specimens for this record. To George L. McKay he is indebted for the accompanying checklist of the author's books, articles and fugitive pieces.

MY STORY OF THE DESIGNS

INTRODUCTION

Whenever I decided to write about the types I have designed since 1896, my intention was to do little more than to prepare a simple, straightforward, more or less chronological list with brief notes about the facts of their making. But, as I have said in the preface to my *Typologia*, "who, once having begun a book, can resist its own invitations—to quote, to comment, to ponder and amplify?" And that is exactly what has happened here.

A number of years ago I realized that the history of my first seventeen or eighteen types had never had serious attention; the greater part of the drawings and sketches for these early attempts had been burned in the fire which, on January 10, 1908, wiped out my printing office and studio in the Parker Building, on Fourth Avenue at Nineteenth Street, New York City, leaving only records of odds and ends at our apartment on West 117th Street.

By taking these meager relics, adding the bits of information that came to me now and then regarding these types, the facts and incidents of their making which remained in memory, I began to prepare notes regarding each type and, as fully as possible, to add information as new matter came to light. I had not at that time any definite idea of the use I might make of these notes nor in fact any reason for them, except to preserve the facts still fresh in recollection. Occasionally for someone who wanted biographical material I would draw on them, but in the main they remained simply a part of my store of material to use for talks, magazine articles, etc.

In the fall of 1942, in response to an invitation from the Typophiles, I began the serious preparation of the present Chap Book. After writing some thirty or more pages of manuscript I was taken ill and work on it of course stopped. During a period of slow convalescence I reviewed in memory the work already done and it occurred to me that here I might properly attempt to clear up some inaccurate statements that have gotten into print, and present, to those who know me only by my work, something also of my aims and ambitions.

For myself personally I do not believe there are any hidden springs in my intellectual development that a psychoanalyst could use to advantage. From the very beginning of a career which began most casually, I have never thought of my work other than as the straightaway, everyday work of the shop, always striving to do each separate job as well as I could, and striving also to do the next job, if possible, better.

As I look back on the events of almost half a century, I maintain that for the greater portion of my work I have attempted not merely to follow precedent, but have tried also to add something of myself. And yet, while adding that something, there has never been any intention of foisting innovations (and by innovations I mean novelties in design) on the reader. It has always been my hope with each new type that the reader might discover in it a new degree of beauty, legibility or distinction, rather than the mere fact that it was just another design.

19

It was never among the dreams of my youth that I would become a writer of sorts, or as has been said "the most *prolific* designer of types of all time," nevertheless it is a source of great satisfaction to me that during my lifetime some of my type creations have enjoyed a popularity never accorded some of the truly great types of the past during the lifetime of *their* designers.

And since this introduction is in a sense an unburdening of my soul, I am constrained to acknowledge here that I have always deplored the fact that the *first* real recognition of my types came from an English writer and English printers, instead of from printers or writers in my own fatherland, and that the acceptance of my types here came only long after their earlier acceptance in England.

It has been my great sorrow too, that I never had a college or university training, a sorrow tempered however by the fact that a college and two universities have honored me with doctorates for my work in type design.

The idea that a designer of types might write a critical commentary on his own work may seem strange. It is unusual, of course, but after all, why not? Who should know better the sources from which his work springs, the influences of its development, the aims and ideals which inspired it, and its excellences or its shortcomings?

In my own case, many articles about me and my work have appeared, a few good—some indifferent. Almost all of them contain slips of the pen; most of them recount obvious facts regarding the types themselves, but seldom get into the record the vicissitudes and the items seemingly of little account, that seemed merely to serve their turn, but which probably influenced the course of life itself.

It seems difficult for biographers to agree on the place of my birth, a fact which never has been a secret in any sense of the word. They persist in crediting various towns, in spite of definite information as to the correct place—Bloomington, Illinois—though they usually get the date, March 8, 1865, correct.

I shall not attempt a complete review of my life, contenting myself with a brief statement of my earliest recollections of any art aspirations or incidents that seem to me to have a bearing on the work I have made my own, confining the account as far as I can to those matters in relation to my own typographic offspring.

I have always felt that an autobiography, usually commonplace, is too often an expression of one sort of egotism which I would never attempt, and so what I set down here of an autobiographical nature is intended merely to present those details of a somewhat checkered career which have to do with the record of my work.

As a student of printing, of type design and the work of the early designers, I have seized with avidity upon stray references as to what manner of men those artists might have been, their methods of work, and particularly their viewpoints regarding their own work. Therefore I feel that what I say here may interest students in later years, as presenting certain facts regarding my own work that are exhibited in the faces of the actual types—facts of which probably I can speak better than another.

My father was a school teacher, later a superintendent of city schools, and a county superintendent of schools when he died. He had been admitted to the bar, and at one time was Judge of the Probate Court. He was the son of a farmer, and was born in a country village in Ohio—Yellow Springs, now the seat of Antioch College. As a boy he was the schoolmate of a boy who later achieved great distinction in political and journalistic life—the late Whitelaw Reid. My father had a number of brothers and sisters, and all (except one) became teachers at some time in their lives, one brother becoming state superintendent of schools for Nebraska.

I have said that I never heard of anyone in our family who ever followed printing as a craft, or showed any artistic tendencies. But when I was only ten years of age I was able to make creditable pencil copies of wood-engravings found in the magazines of the '70's, and strangely enough, after copying one of these carefully, I could make a good facsimile of it from memory. But as I remember, any *creative* instinct at this time seemed absolutely lacking in my artistic make-up.

In 1876, the year of the great Centennial Exposition at Philadelphia, we were living in Bloomington, the little city in Illinois where I had been born eleven years earlier. This particular year sticks out in my memory as the beginning of my art career.

The City Courthouse occupied a square formed by two north-and-south and two east-and-west streets.

Surrounding the Courthouse grounds was a stone curb, maybe a foot or so high. At the southeast corner of the square, one hot summer afternoon, I came across a man sitting just inside the curb on a camp stool, under a large umbrella. In front of him was an ordinary kitchen table on which was fastened a simple wooden contraption with which he was outlining, on paper fastened under it, the enlarged contours of a photograph. It was the first time I had ever seen a pantograph. At one place it carried a point, at another was affixed a pencil or crayon, and as the man guided the point around the outlines of the photograph, the pencil duplicated roughly the movements of the point and reproduced on the paper the lines traced by the point; to these outlines he later added shading and modeling free-hand.

I watched him as the picture developed, entranced. Seeing my interest, he suggested that I, too, could do it. The wonder of it! I could not tear myself away. As I have said, at this time I was already attempting to copy pictures and here was a sure means at hand. How to get one of these wonderful affairs? The price was twenty-five cents—this I knew because the artist sold several right under my very nose. It occurred to me that the errand on which I had been sent was still unperformed and I began to wonder what might happen on my delayed return home. I don't recall that anything serious did happen, but evidently my enthusiastic description of the apparatus, and my plea for the twenty-five cents, won over an obdurate parent—twenty-five cent shinplasters were real sums in those days. Soon I was back to the corner where the artist still was demon-

23

strating his art and wares; the shin-plaster and pantograph exchanged hands. The passage of light through space is a synonym for speed, but I was a serious competitor in getting my new treasure home. With what pride I demonstrated its capabilities to my father and mother!

Several years ago, while driving from New York to Chicago, I suggested to my wife that we detour and take in Bloomington, where I would show her the cottage on East Jefferson Street where I was born. I didn't, however, as the house itself had disappeared; but I did find the site, and also I was able to point out proudly the place on the stone curb where so many years before I had watched the artist demonstrate.

A year or two later we moved to Macomb, Illinois, where there were many potteries, mostly making the simpler things like jugs, jars, crocks, flower pots, etc. I used frequently to watch the potter at his whirling wheel driven by digs of his foot on a treadle, a batch of wet clay on the revolving table with which he would "throw" a jug, then attach a handle, and set it aside to dry and glaze before burning. Even in those youthful days handicraft had a fascination for me. I watched the potter just as I had watched a workman in a Bloomington chair factory turn wooden table legs, stair banisters, chair rounds, and so on, at a lathe a few years earlier.

In Bloomington, when I was eleven years of age, an old lady used to get from this chair factory the wooden frames for chair seats, drilled around the edges with holes in which to insert the long strips of cane which, when woven, formed the seat. She

24

offered to instruct any of us young fellows how to "cane" a chair in return for two completed seats done for her—which she, of course, would turn into the factory for whatever they paid for such work. Under her instruction I "caned" two seats for her, and afterward did several for our own home and others for the neighbors. Although it is over three-score years since I tried my hand at it, I believe I can "cane" a chair today, the processes are so clear in my mind.

When I was about fifteen, we had moved to Butler, Illinois. I saw an advertisement for a scroll-saw and lathe offered by the then popular boys' magazine, *The Youth's Companion*. It cost $10.00. To earn the $10.00 I became janitor of the grammar school of which my father was principal. That I got the job was probably an early case of nepotism, since my only recommendation for it was the fact that I was the principal's son. Anyway, I got the lathe; it was small, and inefficient except for the simplest work, but it did exert a marked influence on my later work—it fostered and crystallized a liking for the mechanical work I was to come back to many years later.

Incidentally, a few years ago while spending the day with Bruce Rogers, at New Fairfield, Connecticut, I was delighted when he showed me a little lathe *exactly* like the one which I had worked so hard to get more than fifty-odd years before. If he told me where he got it I have forgotten, but it did bring back pleasant memories. He offered to let me have it when I told him of my earlier experience, but to my everlasting credit I did not take advantage of his kind offer.

25

We remained about two years at Butler and then father was made superintendent of the Shelbyville, Illinois, schools and in 1881 we moved to that interesting little city on the banks of the Okaw. The class of students was unusually good and a number of my school mates I still correspond with and occasionally see. A number of well-known people hail from there: Augusta Cottlow, the pianist, was born there; George R. Wendling, known as the "silver-tongued orator," had his start in Shelbyville; Charles Wagner, the impresario, now in New York, and L. E. Behymer, for many years impresario in Los Angeles; Robert Root, painter, all hail from Shelbyville. Frank Wendling, the brother of George, was my classmate. He too, could orate with all the gestures of a professional speaker and at the graduation exercises my simple oratorical efforts must have seemed weak and colorless in comparison with his more showy exhibition. He and I were the only boys in a class of ten or twelve.

Nell Davis, my first sweetheart, helped me cut more than 3,000 letters out of a maroon-colored flock wall-paper. Out of these I formed the ten commandments and other Bible bits, with which the church trustees *allowed* me to decorate the Presbyterian Sunday School room. They had just had the church painted and the school room papered. I noticed, one morning during the Sunday School class (Nell's mother was in charge of my class), that after the completion of the painting and papering, there were a number of panels formed by the high wainscoting and the picture rail between windows. I noticed also that there were just ten spaces between

26

the picture rail and the ceiling—why not put the ten commandments in these spaces, to form a sort of frieze around the room?

Later on, and quite likely that very Sunday afternoon, I outlined some letters of the alphabet about three inches high that could be cut out without too much difficulty. I recall their shapes perfectly, and as Bernard Lewis in his *The Man Behind the Type*, says, they were more or less similar to a later type I made which I called "Ornate." I imagine my recollection of the Shelbyville work may unconsciously have influenced me in the making of Ornate.

The next thing was to get permission to do the work. Probably the fact that I offered to do it without charge was an inducement in part to bring the desired permission. As the trestles and paper boards used for his papering by Mr. Blankinship, who was doing the decorating, were still on the premises, it was a simple matter for me, by using his equipment —after cutting the letters for one of the Commandments out of the wall-paper I had selected for its color, etc.—to arrange them in words and sentences on the paper board, properly spaced to fill the actual length available for the panel, and then, after striking a chalk line in the panel, to paste them down as laid out on the board.

The job was simple, but there are an awful lot of letters in the ten commandments. However, I soon developed a technique for cutting them so that all the A's would be similar, and so on with each letter of the alphabet.

I drew the complete original alphabet, each letter of the proper size, on a sheet of stiff wrapping-paper begged from the dry-goods store, the proprietor of which was himself a trustee and member of the church and cognizant of the work I was about to attempt.

This same store at one time had exhibited in one of its show windows a banner of red sateen I had made for a local organization—a polite order of vigilantes to prevent horse stealing (we were a rural community) called the Rosehill Horse Association. That may not be the exact title—strange too, that I shouldn't remember; it was only sixty years ago—but I can see in my mind's eye the exact appearance of that banner. It was about 2½ x 3½ feet in size. Part of the name I painted in gold letters in a curved line in the upper part, over a painting of a trotting horse which I had copied out of an old type-specimen book, with the balance of the name of the concern in a straight line just below the picture. As the work of a local boy it attracted considerable attention—and some criticism—from the local jeweler who set up as art critic. I had painted the horse in motion—a grey horse it was—and of course I didn't make the hoofs of the horse as clear and distinct as they would be shown were the animal standing still. This indistinctness, which I thought suggested movement, was the principal point of the jeweler's criticism—he wanted his details clearcut and well defined, otherwise it wasn't art.

I previously had designed and lettered a large screen for the only billiard parlor the town afforded. It pleased the proprietor very much until I casually mentioned that I wanted three dollars for it, whereupon his interest waned. It was this same summer that I exhibited at the County Fair a pencil drawing which I had copied from a wood-engraving in a magazine, and, to my surprise, it brought an award of three dollars.

But to get back to the Sunday School work: after drawing the letters on the thick wrapping paper, I proceeded to cut them out carefully with a sharp knife, using them as templates to outline the letters on the back of the wall-paper. They were reversed, of course, so the letters themselves would be upright when cut out. The magnitude of the work began to strike in at this point. Nevertheless, I cut enough letters for one or two of the commandments, pasted them in position and waited for Sunday's verdict as to the project. The effect must have been pleasing as I was not stopped. Then my friend Nell offered to help me cut out the letters. After the first few attempts she did the work effectively and quickly, making my work much easier and giving me more time to devote to the arrangement of the texts.

After the commandments were put up, the bareness of larger panels formed by wainscoting and picture-rail between windows seemed to me to invite treatment and without waiting for permission to decorate them, I inserted Bible texts, using also, in addition to my regular cut-out letters, some ornamental initials I copied out of an old type-specimen book borrowed from the leading newspaper office. These I cut out of gilt paper; and for some of the panels where the arrangement seemed to me to demand a border, I made one by cutting strips of gilt paper to surround the texts selected.

At the back of the altar platform was quite a large

panel and I concentrated on it, using initials and border lines, to present the Beatitudes. I again waited Sunday's verdict. It seemed to be approval; and I went ahead, filling all the available spaces, with the teachers suggesting texts from which I selected the ones that seemed best adapted (and easiest to do) in the spaces presented. I think I must have worked some five or six weeks before finishing the large room.

Just at this time the father of my friend Behymer, a contractor and builder, asked me to go to the little neighboring town of Bethany where he was erecting a church. The church, of course, could not afford real stained-glass windows, but he figured that if the glass were pounced over with white lead, it would give the window a frosted or ground glass effect. I suggested that I could also stencil on each one a simple border design in color that would better simulate the stained-glass effect. This had not occurred to him and he was a bit dubious. So I planned a border and on a large pane of glass which I "frosted" with white paint, I applied the stencil border in blue paint. The effect was good—at a little distance one could almost imagine it actually was stained glass, especially the country layman who maybe had never seen any real stained glass. Mr. Behymer was delighted and I went to Bethany. I had some friends there whom I had visited previously now and then too—there was a girl named Annie Logan who probably was the real reason for those visits. I arranged to board with her parents; Mr. Logan was a lumber merchant and I paid part of my board and lodging by painting for him a long sign for his business place. After I had finished the "stained-glass" work which took longer than it should (probably on account of Annie) I returned to Shelbyville and found the church people had in the meantime given my mother a check for twenty dollars for me to show their appreciation of my work in the Sunday school room, and a little later, after hearing comments of visitors, the trustees insisted on giving me another check for twenty dollars.

Strange to say, those letters remained on the walls for over twenty years, when the church was redecorated, a metal ceiling put up and my work obliterated by being painted over. In 1923 or '24 Mr. Robert Ballou, then of Chicago, was writing an article about me for *The American Mercury*, and Mitchell Kennerley, reading advance proofs of the article in which Ballou had mentioned my Shelbyville work, telegraphed to the church people suggesting that if any of my work had simply been covered up, he would pay for any labor necessary to bring it to light so that it might be photographed, and that he would also pay for the restoration of the room. The new painting, however, had so completely ruined my earlier work that it was impossible to restore it for photographing.

It was about this time, 1884, that our local baker got a new delivery wagon and asked me if I could paint his name on each side of it. I did, using what today would be called a sans-serif letter—then it was known as "block" letter. I remember clearly that I made each letter the same width and put the same amount of measured space between each. I don't know now how I made my I's, but possibly the name didn't call for any (I don't remember the name

31

of the baker); so maybe I was saved some embarrassment, as it would have been difficult to make an "I" as wide as an "H" and still be much of an "I."

Later that year I went out to Dakota territory to join my father who had taken up the real estate business.

By this time I was working with him in the office and frequently laid out for printing some of the numerous blanks we required. These I had printed at a nearby town by a printer who did especially good work for that era of typographic monstrosities. Even then, unconsciously, I was developing a flair for typographic arrangement. I purchased a sort of duplicating device which worked (as I now know) on the principle of lithography and with it I executed bits of printing of the blanks and advertisements we needed, and which I drew and lettered.

Life was humdrum enough, but fortunately there were in the little Dakota town quite a number of young men and girls—about the same age as myself, so that we managed to have a good time. Summers were hot and winters cold. I remember well the great blizzard of '88, when over two hundred people lost their lives in Iowa, Nebraska and Dakota—I, myself, was out in it for several hours, and for readers who have never experienced a western blizzard I am free to say I never want to see another.

I spent the next year or two, first in Minneapolis, where I was cashier for a big department store, then in Springfield, Illinois; and finally, in January, 1890, I landed in Chicago.

Since leaving Dakota I had given no thought to typography. My first Chicago job was that of private secretary for a financial broker, who had become acquainted with me through acting as agent for the sale of Dakota farm mortgages negotiated by my father and me. Since he was familiar with some of the layouts I had made, he had me arrange and have printed for him the prospectuses of his clients, and in this way I came into contact with several Chicago printers.

I remained with him for some months until I got a position with a real estate firm, a position which I held all through the World's Fair and after. Leaving that office I went from one job to another—one with a book concern which specialized in second-hand school books.

At this time I really began to be interested in books as books, in terms of their physical appearance. Fortunately, through regular visits to the large bookstore of A. C. McClurg & Co., I became acquainted with George Millard, who was in charge of the rare book department, and his assistant, Mr. Chandler. Millard noticed my interest in certain productions of the then new private presses—Kelmscott, Vale, Eragny, Doves—and he went out of his way to show me the new books from these presses as they came in. Thus I came to know something of them. I studied the types used in them and now and then I would buy a book about books, like Gordon Duff's *Early Printed Books*, and Alfred Pollard's *Early Illustrated Books* (which, by the way, I still have). I couldn't afford many, however.

After leaving the second-hand book shop, I had one or two short-lived jobs, and the last one having petered out, I was left more or less (mostly more) on my uppers. One day I ran into C. Lauron Hooper, an old friend, who asked what I was doing. When I told him "nothing," he immediately offered to help me get started again, and asked what I would like to do. My occasional work at writing and laying out advertisements came to mind and I said "if I had the money I would start a little printing plant to produce advertising booklets." This, mind you, at a time when I hardly knew which end of a type was the printing end. He said he could furnish a small amount of cash if I would contribute my time. Thus the "Booklet Press" was born, but it almost died aborning, for an early commission from a printing broker required new type and thus put us to considerable expense—while the broker who had ordered the work very kindly collected from the customers the amount due us, but by some curious twist of his mentality didn't think it necessary to pay *us* any of it. We weathered the blow, however, and continued work. A lucky connection with Stone & Kimball brought us the then new "Chap Book" to print.

We had been recommended to the publishers by my friend W. Irving Way, and this connection, I now realize, brought about in me all unaware a new conception of art and literature—by the back door, as it were. I learned something from the exponents of the New Hedonism, although I must confess I didn't know exactly just what it was all about. Yet, in spite of my ignorance, I sensed something back of it all that for me raised typography to a higher plane than mere commercialism. The "Chap Book" opened my eyes to a new world; it brought me into contact through its pages with the writers and artists then high in the literary firmament. In this way I began my work in that period of transition known as *le fin du siecle:* I belong to the Beardsley period, although actually never a part of it.

Perhaps I may be permitted to interpolate here a quotation from an 1896 magazine which is inconsequential in itself but which, when I came across it while working on the present chronicle, was interesting and almost prophetic to me.

By 1896 I had already become interested in typographical matters and bought such books and magazines on the subject as my meager means permitted. Among my accumulations of typographic odds and ends was a little magazine called *Poster Lore.* This was published by Frederic Thoreau Singleton in the last place in the world where one would look for a bit of "dilettantism"—Kansas City—and was printed "for art students and latter day enthusiasts." This particular number is dated September, 1896, and presented articles mostly about the poster designers of that day: Ethel Reed, C. W. Traver, Will Bradley, Edward Penfield, Claude Fayette Bragdon, Will Carqueville and others.

One article by the publisher about his own "amateur print-shop at the Red-Pale" contained this paragraph: "I can remember with what extravagant enthusiasm and appreciation the promoters of a well-known bibelot in this frontier town carried to their printer a copy of the Chap Book, as an parcel of things new, pleasing and desirable in Typography." He continued, "Here I am reminded of the printing experience of Mr. F. W. Goudy, Chicago, who in connection with Mr. C. L. Hooper, started the

Camelot Press two or three years ago, which establishment, I believe, at one time printed the Chap Book. Although totally uninstructed in the art of printing, Mr. Goudy took to it naturally, achieved considerable success and turned out work of decided individuality. As to what Mr. Goudy will accomplish as a designer, it is hard to predict. He does not attempt to cover the entire field of design, but confines himself to such special work as initial blocks, page ornaments, book covers, etc."

Some twenty years ago I became acquainted with Mr. Singleton personally, although I have since lost track of him. I wonder whether he remembers what he wrote so many years ago, or if he would have come close to the facts had he ventured a prediction!

In the same issue of *Poster Lore* is recorded the death of William Morris.

I finally sold my interest in the little press. When we took on the "Chap Book" to print, I had decided that "Booklet Press" wasn't a good name for it, considering its now wider field, and I changed the name to "Camelot Press." After selling my interest in the Camelot Press to George Leland Hunter, who at that time was the foreign rewrite editor on the *Chicago Tribune*, I began looking for other work. The purchaser of my interest didn't find the going as easy as he anticipated and in a few months the sheriff helped him close out the Camelot Press.

And this brings me up to my first attempt at type designing. That it would turn out to be my future profession was not within my wildest dreams.

CAMELOT
[Design No. 1]

WHILE operating the Camelot Press, my associate C. Lauron Hooper and I had working for us a young man named Berne Nadall. He was employed to set type, but as a type compositor he wasn't much better than myself. He was, however, something of a decorative designer and did the odds and ends of such work we needed. When I left the Press I remembered his work and tried my own hand at design also. For the want of anything to do, since I was as yet unemployed, one evening, in my small bedroom on Michigan Avenue, I idly drew an alphabet of capital letters in pencil, each letter about five-eighths of an inch high; and as letters drawn on paper are useless in themselves, I sent the sheet to the Dickinson Type Foundry in Boston, from which I had earlier purchased type now and then for the Camelot Press. As the drawing took less than an hour to do, I asked if the drawing was worth five dollars; and to my great surprise, in the course of a week or two, a letter of acceptance came enclosing a check for ten dollars!

Later the Foundry added a lower-case to my capitals, but by whom it was drawn I do not know. I

ABCDEFGHIJKLMNOPQ
RJTUVWXYZ&.,';:!?-

$1234567890

first saw the type in use while I was working in Detroit in 1897, and the type is still in occasional use even now. A year or so ago, when I was in Atlanta, I was the guest of my old friend Richard McArthur, at one time the advertising manager for the Barnhart Bros. & Spindler Type Foundry in Chicago. He gave me an early illustrated pamphlet about Camelot which had been issued by the Boston branch, but with some changes in the design. I was very glad to have it, as my copies had been burned in the fire in the Parker Building.

UNNAMED
[Design No. 2]

ENCOURAGED by the ready acceptance of my drawings for the "Camelot," a cap font, I attempted
another design—this time caps and lower-case. It
was an alphabet of slightly inclined letters, not
really an italic, as at that time my study of lettering
had not reached very far into the traditional side of
type design. My work was largely intuitional, if
such a term can be applied to type design, and I did
not then realize that the "italicness" of a font of
type is not a mere inclination of the roman form,
but rather that an italic must exhibit a fundamental
character of its own, with a disciplined freedom of
drawing and an exuberance not possible (or desirable) in the roman forms.

Anyway, I worked diligently at this face, inking
in the letters, which were about three or four inches
high and drawn on slips of paper, which as I remember were about six by fourteen inches in size. This
design too was sent to the Dickinson Foundry in
Boston. A little later it came back with the word
that if I cared to make a few indicated changes the
foundry would consider its purchase, and asking also
that a price be set. The suggested changes were made,
but before returning the revised drawings to Boston,
I showed them to a new-found friend—Clarence
Marder of Marder, Luse & Co., type founders, to
whom I had previously sold some drawings for a
page of type ornaments. I asked Marder's advice as
to the amount I might safely charge Boston for the
design and he kindly named a higher figure than I, in

my ignorance of such things, had dared to suggest. Marder liked the design and in substance said, "if Boston didn't take it, Marder, Luse & Co. would." Boston did take it and sent a check for the modest sum asked. Whatever became of the drawings I do not know—they never appeared as type. Maybe the foundry was merely encouraging "the young idea how to shoot." This was early in 1897.

A "DISPLAY" ROMAN
[Design No. 3]

MARDER's suggestion that he might buy the italic design, if Boston did not, gave me the idea of making another design and offering it to him. At this time I was becoming more and more interested in decorative design, and was reading with avidity each month the issues of *The London Studio*,* which showed the work of designers like Harold Nelson, R. Anning Bell, C. T. Voysey, Walter Crane, Aubrey Beardsley, and other English artists, and I soon learned to recognize their styles.

It never occurred to me then that some day I might actually meet some of these men, as I later did. Frequently, their designs contained lettering, and one of them showed a letter which I thought I might turn into a type. Using it as a basis I made drawings—which I proudly (and hopefully) submitted to Marder. He did not know that upon his decision my landlady would receive what was due her for room rent, and I could take my belongings and leave for Detroit, where I had just secured a position as cashier of a farm publication. Marder suggested that if my price were not *too high* he would take the drawings and *pay* for them. I named the same amount I had charged for the Boston design I had shown him. This I thought was good policy, as it was the exact amount *he* himself had suggested I charge the Boston concern when his advice was asked. He purchased the drawings at my figure!

*I still have Vol. I, No. 1, with the first mention of the work of Aubrey Beardsley by my friend, the late Joseph Pennell.

41

This design isn't very clear in my mind after forty-five years; my recollection is that it was a display letter leaning to the bold side. I can't imagine it was very distinguished, but Marder told me only a few years ago that he remembered it as "pretty good." We must remember that original type designs were not at that time (1897) regular items of purchase by a type foundries; most of their types were produced by their own punch-cutters, and were usually mere variations only of the types of other foundries. At any rate, this particular design was lost in the shuffle and has never appeared. Probably the difficulty of knowing whether a type will sell or not by merely looking at the drawings, without actually cutting the face, had something to do with its nonappearance. The cost of the design itself is but a fraction of the final expense of producing a new type.

By this time I had almost made up my mind that designing type was a precarious business, even though my first three designs had sold, so when I was asked by the publisher of *The Michigan Farmer*, a weekly farm magazine published in Detroit, to become its cashier and bookkeeper, I decided to play safe and accept the position. Marder paid me promptly for the drawings I had submitted to him, and I was able to pay my few debts and leave for Detroit.

As the farm magazine was printed on its own premises I began to spend idle time in the print shop, occasionally laying out some of the magazine's advertising. One of its regular advertisers who lived in Detroit used to come in frequently and we beca me quite well acquainted. This customer, Alfred Zen ner, noticing me working on a layout, asked me to do something for him to make his advertising more distinctive. One of his commissions, a pamphlet cover, brought from him a criticism of some lettering—a criticism which probably influenced me more in my lettering work than any other single thing. He remarked: "You are not very strong on lowercase, are you?" His remark put me on my mettle and I began then seriously to study roman letter forms. This was about 1898.

After forty-six years it is evident that his simple criticism was, to me, a matter of importance. I have no doubt today that it was the thing that influenced the entire future course of my life; it was not apparent then, of course, but it did really suggest the new path of thought and study I then began to follow.

Some months after I had gone to Detroit, I was delighted to receive a large pamphlet issued by the Kellogg Newspaper Union of Chicago, set in capital letters—my very first letters which I had sent to the Boston Foundry in 1896. The Foundry, without suggestion on my part, had named the type "Camelot" remembering, probably, my previous purchases of type for the Camelot Press. By this time the Dickinson foundry had become a branch of the American Type Founders Company.

While I was still working for *The Michigan Farmer* I drew for Walter Marder, the brother of Clarence, and who was at that time at the Central Type Foundry, St. Louis, the DeVinne roman.

DE VINNE ROMAN
[Design No. 4]

WALTER MARDER asked me to take the then famous DeVinne display type and make a book face of it. As I did not know the original inspiration for the face, I probably made as successful a transcription as anyone could and still retain the DeVinne character in a book weight type; it did not prove as acceptable to printers, however, as the founders hoped. The foundry carried it in their specimen books for some years before finally dropping it. Long after I had delivered my drawings, I learned that the same commission had been given the *original* designer (whose name escapes me) of the DeVinne face who, however, could not get away from the type that inspired it, and in his drawings he lost entirely the DeVinne character, his lettering suggesting only the Elzevir, on which he had based his design.

THE TIMES WHEN ADVERTISERS INSISTED UPON A HEAVY BLACKFACE OR Gothic in displaying advertisements are past. The educational forces that are at work in printing have wrought so well that there is widespread appreciation in evidence of the beauty and value of the refined and $1234567890 neat light faces

In 1899 I lost my job as bookkeeper in Detroit, and returned to Chicago. Realizing that as a book-keeper I was not of the caliber that develops actuaries or chartered accountants, I decided to abandon that field for good; but what to do? since by this time I had a wife; and food, raiment and housing were strongly indicated. While working in Detroit I had at odd times tried my hand at lettering and minor decoration. I even had made a set of ornamental initials for my friend Clarence Marder (their ultimate destination unknown), and had drawn a cover for *The Inland Printer*, and so on; it seemed then that designing and lettering were the logical things to practice. No sooner thought than done—sublime confidence, or complete asininity, according to the way you look at it.

By making up a few drawings as specimens, which I submitted bravely to A. C. McClurg & Company, Lyon & Healy, Herbert S. Stone & Company, Thomas B. Mosher, Way & Williams, and others, commissions gradually came. I recall that Charles H. Sergel, a Chicago book publisher, was the first to employ me, and I made several book covers for him.

I have never since experienced the thrill that was mine at the sight of a show window of the McClurg book store, piled high with copies of George Ade's *Fables in Slang*, showing the cover which I had designed for Herbert Stone & Company, the publishers of the book.

After settling myself in Chicago I began seriously to try to get commissions for any sort of commercial designs that required lettering and simple decorative features. While in Detroit, I had opened up corre-

45

spondence with Thomas B. Mosher of Portland, Maine, and as early as 1899 I had done three or four book-cover designs for his "Vest-Pocket" Series, one of which, an edition of Omar Khayyam, attracted quite a bit of attention. This was followed by three other books: *Sonnets from the Portuguese*, *Laus Veneris*, and *Quattrocentisteria*, all in the same format (size 2½ by 5⅞ inches), but with a different cover design on each, although all of the covers had the same general character. Mosher later issued other items using the same designs. Of course I turned to him now, soliciting other work, and he gave me several small commissions.

In 1899, I had also done several book covers for Mosher's "Old World Series." For these he specified lettering for my designs to match or harmonize with the lettering on the title-pages, which had been done for him by Bruce Rogers. This was the first I had heard of Rogers, and who he was, or what his standing in the art world might be, I didn't learn until two or three years later. Then my friend W. Irving Way, of Way & Williams, showed me a book-cover drawing which he said was by "the great designer, Bruce Rogers." To do what Mosher asked I found impossible; Rogers already had developed a style that was his own and I could merely approximate it in appearance. Mosher found my work "mannered," and I did but little more for him.

I was pleased, however, when I moved to New York City in 1906, to meet him in person in the book-publishing office of Mitchell Kennerley. Mosher was very kind to me and I was his guest one evening at the Grolier Club, where I met for the first time some of the celebrities of the book world. Thirteen years later, in 1920, I myself became a member of the club and I still retain my membership, one of the bright spots of my literary and artistic life. I have met there such men as Walter Gillis, Charles Scribner, Dr. Kunz, Seymour de Ricci and Dr. Rosenbach. It has been my great privilege to speak there on several occasions, the last time on the evening of April 22, 1943, at an exhibition of my own work.

The work I succeeded in obtaining from A. C. McClurg & Company, Marshall Field & Company, and from some of Chicago's other department stores, attracted the attention of Frank Holme, a newspaper artist of marked ability and versatility. He conceived the idea of establishing a "School of Illustration," and invited a number of leading Chicago illustrators to join his teaching staff. In addition to the artists, he asked several well-known men in other lines to serve as advisors. He surprised me one day by asking if I would teach lettering and design in the school. He couldn't promise much remuneration, but he thought an association with men like Edgar Cameron, Will Carqueville, John T. McCutcheon, Joe and Frank Leyendecker, Fred Mulhaupt, Ray Long, William Jean Beauley, E. N. Thayer and J. M. Gaspard might help me in my own struggle for existence. He was getting out a little booklet to advertise the school and I remember the pleasure he took in showing me a proof of the cover, which Joe Leyendecker had drawn on the stone for lithographing. I immediately offered to letter the title page. The little booklet contained brief accounts of the work of the instructors, with a portrait of each.

Well, I began work as an instructor and it was the best thing I ever did. I had to study harder than any student who came under my tutelage, but I managed to keep at least *one* lesson ahead of the class. I worried a good bit about my progress when I would notice Frank listening to me at times as I talked to my class, and I wondered how soon the axe would fall. One day he surprised me by inviting me to luncheon and during the meal casually remarked that he had been following my work at the school; he thought I had made my course interesting, and "would I be angry with him if he gave me fifty dollars?" I could have kissed him.

It was in the school that I came in contact with the late letterer and type designer, Oswald Cooper, a most lovable character. Here I also became acquainted with William A. Dwiggins, who had been attending the Art Institute to study illustration but wasn't getting on as well as he wished. One day he visited my class and heard me talk regarding decorative design and lettering—talk which, he says, opened up a new concept of design to him. He left the Institute and came over to the School of Illustration. Several artists who later achieved worldwide distinction got their start in art in the Frank Holme School. Harry Hirshfield, the well known radio commentator, was also a pupil who showed great ability as an art student. Alas! what the radio gained, art lost.

While still teaching in the Holme School I met W. W. Denslow, a newspaper artist. Denslow conceived the idea of illustrating and lettering *Mother Goose*, to be published by McClure, Phillips & Company of New York. He had lettered the title page and one or two of the jingles, when he realized that as a letterer he was a much better illustrator. I think it must have been Frank Holme who suggested to him that maybe I could more easily do the lettering he required. He came to me and I said I would letter one or two pages for him and he could then decide whether he wished me to do the work. I did the "Humpty-Dumpty sat on a wall" page, which pleased him. After looking over the copy, I found a number of the rhymes required only four to six lines of lettering, a few longer, and I named a price of two dollars each page for the work. He was amazed —he had expected to pay much more for the lettering. Another thing he liked was the rapidity with which I turned it out (I needed the money).

Later, Denslow brought Elbert Hubbard of the Roycroft Press, with whom he at one time had worked in Aurora, New York, to see me, and I did a number of bookplates for Hubbard, for which he solicited orders through his advertisements in his *Philistine* magazine. Some years ago in a copy of *The Book Lover*, a quarterly magazine, I saw reproductions of a number of the bookplates I had made for Hubbard, bearing the captions "designed by Elbert Hubbard," though each one bore my initial "G." Hubbard went down with the *Lusitania*—as did my friend Herbert Stone.

But to get back to Denslow's *Mother Goose*: To do the lettering expeditiously, I developed a form of letter at once distinctive and, for me, easy to execute more or less rapidly. The ascenders and descenders were short, the height of the short letters like a, o, c,

49

e, m, n, etc., was noticeably high in relation to the ascenders and descenders. To my surprise, a little later on, the Inland Type Foundry of St. Louis, without consultation with me, brought out a new type copied—not inspired—from my Denslow lettering, and added insult to injury by naming it "Hearst."*

Denslow always signed his work "Den," with a hippocampus (sea horse) in silhouette in connection with the "Den." He came to see me in the Parker Building before the fire, but later I lost track of him.

The Chicago printer who made the book for Denslow told me that often his six- or seven-year-old son sat on his lap evenings and the boy would go over each page of the *Mother Goose*, reading the jingle aloud, and when he came to the colophon: "The verses in this book have been hand-lettered by Fred. W. Goudy," he would read that too, as one of the Mother Goose rhymes. My copy of the book burned in the fire of 1908, but a dear friend who was one of my pupils later at the Art Students League in New York gave me a copy on finding that I had none.

Then, for several years, type design apparently occupied me not at all. Whether I made no attempts at getting type commissions, or whether I was too busy at my regular designing work to think of types, is not clear after the lapse of years. It is possible, however, that the Pabst and Powell types (later described) were drawn during this time. My facility and prolificity in lettering already had attracted the attention of Marshall Field & Company, Hart Schaffner & Marx, Lyon & Healey, Kuppenheimer & Company and others.

*Note Powell type, No. 7, for fuller details of this lettering.

My work with A. C. McClurg & Company brought me more or less into contact with the rare book department then in charge of George Millard and, as I have already mentioned, he noticed my interest in the printing of Morris, Ricketts,* and Cobden-Sanderson, and very kindly went out of his way to show me the new things received. It was the types in these books and their use that decided me to make a deeper study of early printing and to buy as many books about printing as I could—books I still have, and treasure, too. Cobden-Sanderson's *Ideal Book*, which I could ill afford but could not resist buying, was one of the items that later influenced the founding of the Village Press. I had to sell it, however, to help fight the wolf at the door, and it was not until a year or so ago that a dear friend, knowing the story of this particular item, bought a copy as a Christmas present to me.

*Charles Ricketts, one of the proprietors of the Vale Press, had designed the Vale type and it was this type in the *Poems of Sir John Suckling* that really inspired my study of private types.

PABST ROMAN

[Design No. 5]

WHILE I was pursuing my avocation in Chicago, some lettering of advertisements for the Pabst Brewing Company, which I had done for the advertising manager, Joseph Kathrens, and placed through the J. Walter Thompson agency, attracted the attention of Mr. Powell, advertising manager for the department store of Schlesinger & Mayer. He asked me if that particular lettering could be done into type. Drawings were made and delivered to him and paid for. Powell's firm had not realized (nor did I) the amount involved necessary to produce a new type, and decided not to incur the expense of cutting matrices. Powell later approached the American Type Founders Company, who cut a number of sizes, giving Schlesinger & Mayer exclusive use of the face in the newspapers of Chicago for a certain period, after which the design became the property of the foundry and was offered generally to printers.

A B C D E F G H I J K L M
N O P Q R S T U V W X
Y Z a b c d e f g h i j k l m n o p q r s t
u v w x y z *The and & of* Æ Œ
£ $ ﬆ ( ] ‐ ? . : ; , ! ` 1 2 3 4 5 6 7 8 9 0

I objected to calling the type "Powell" and asked permission of Colonel Fred Pabst to name it "Pabst," and the Colonel graciously consented. The type is still in use. My friend Lucian Bernhard, the eminent designer, regards Pabst as one of my *best* designs! And amazingly enough, it was copied abroad under the name "Der Original Haarlemer Type"!

PABST ITALIC
[Design No. 6]

Not long afterward, in 1903, the American Type
Founders Company commissioned me to draw an
italic to accompany the Pabst Roman, and this I did.
I remember particularly the interest I took in watch-
ing the making of the patterns for this type by
Robert Wiebking, who engraved the matrices for the
foundry. As it was a letter characterized by a freedom
of outline which followed my hand lettering, he had
considerable difficulty in preserving the subtle ins
and outs of my freehand drawing without undue
exaggeration of them. I remember also that the
foundry paid me $100. for the design, an unheard-of
figure for a type design in those days.

A B C D E F G H I J K L
M N O P Q R S T U V
W X Y Z a b c d e f g h i j k l m
n o p q r s t u v w x y z A B D G
M N P R T Qu & $ £ fi ff fl
ffi ffl ? ! ' ; : - ' . 1 2 3 4 5 6 7 8 9 0

POWELL
[Design No. 7]

ABOUT the time of cutting the Pabst Italic, Powell
left Schlesinger & Mayer to become advertising
manager for Mandel Brothers, another large department store. Still type-minded, he asked if I would
design a type for his advertising there. Of course, it
must be different from Pabst, and yet have the same
quality of freedom and spontaneity. Some years before this, as I have told on an earlier page, I had
hand-lettered for W. W. Denslow the verses of
Mother Goose, which Mr. Denslow had illustrated.
This letter was distinctive and unlike anything in
use in those days. I have also told how it attracted
the attention of the Inland Type Foundry of St.
Louis, who, without bothering to acquire rights of
reproduction, made it into type, and—horror of
horrors—named it "Hearst"! The main features of
that letter were the short ascenders and descenders
with high middles, that is, such lower-case letters as

A B C D E F G H I J K L M
N O P Q R S T U V W
X Y Z & Æ Œ . , ' ; : ! ? -
a b c d e f g h i j k l m n o
p q r s t u v w x y z æ œ
fi ff fl $ 1 2 3 4 5 6 7 8 9 0 £

m, n, o occupied at least half the body. The appropriation of my stock in trade, as it were, by the foundry, necessitated my developing another form of letter for my own advertising work. I went to the other extreme and developed a letter with long ascenders and short middles—it was this new letter that later became "Pabst" type.* For Powell, now, I designed a letter unlike either Hearst or Pabst by "splitting the difference" between them, that is the height of middles, weight of stems, etc., and presenting some minor differences in handling. Powell submitted the new type design to the Keystone Type Foundry of Philadelphia, who issued it, but what the foundry's arrangement with Powell was, I do not know. I made, however, no objection to the foundry naming it "Powell," as he wished.

I suggested to the Keystone Foundry that I would like to draw an italic for the "Powell," and they *almost* agreed to the suggestion—but they "were not quite ready to do so yet." Later, ignoring my suggestion, they put out an italic designed probably in their own art rooms; at least I did no more toward it than the logotypes "Th," "of," "and," which I had furnished with the drawings for the Roman, and which the foundry used as a basis for its cutting of the Italic.

And now we reach the beginning of my long list of types intended primarily for book printing.

*It has come to my attention recently that the son of Mr. Powell claims his father *designed* both the Pabst and Powell letters, but the story herein presents the actual facts of their making. Mr. Powell merely commissioned their design.

VILLAGE
[Design No. 8]

THE Village type came (rather indirectly) to be the private design of the Village Press and continued as such for a number of years. In 1903, I was doing free-lance designing, and had received a commission from Kuppenheimer & Company, one of my regular customers, to design a type for use in their advertising. As I have said in the little book, *The Story of The Village Type*, published (1933) at the Press of the Wooly Whale:

"The commission . . . was welcomed, and I began the work, taking suggestions for my forms more or less from the types of Jenson, as exhibited in Morris' Golden type, the Doves, Montaigne, Merrymount, and types of that ilk. What an ancestry for an advertising face!

"In due time the drawings were completed, submitted to Mr. Weinstock, advertising manager for Kuppenheimer's, and thoroughly approved by him. The question then arose regarding the cost of producing matrices, and while the figure I quoted him was less than half what similar work today would cost, the total expense seemed too much for the treasurer of the clothing firm, who probably figured he was 'buying a pig in a poke' anyway. After discussing ways and means with Mr. Weinstock, Kuppenheimer's finally decided to pay me a nominal sum for my time, and the firm returned the drawings."

Later in the year, the Village Press was established at Park Ridge, Illinois, by Will Ransom and myself. The reclaimed Kuppenheimer drawings, with revisions, were used as the basis for a private type of the Press. The announcement read:

"The design seems based on an early Italian model, but Mr. Goudy disclaims any conscious intention of imitation, rather having evolved it letter by letter as ideas came, taking some of the best modern private faces . . . with critical and careful consideration, selecting and adopting those points in each which appealed to him, making changes, and with one idea finally in mind throughout, that of considering each letter as a pen letter reduced to type with all limitations of material and use as type."

Will Ransom, in his *Private Presses and Their Books*, says that the Village type "contained elements of drawing, subtle curves and delicate joinings, fresh and new and strangely interesting. It was not copied from nor based upon any previous letter, though it had something of a fifteenth-century Italian air about it. One essence it had was in being drawn entirely free-hand,* a startling innovation in those days when mechanical accuracy was the *sine qua non* of all type, at least in this country."

This design, it is said, "shows Mr. Goudy's early genius for lettering. While he frankly acknowledges the sources of his design, the result was unlike any of them. The type, while carrying good color, escapes the somberness of Morris' Golden, for example, and the unpleasant ruggedness of some other contemporary Italian renderings. It has an individualistic feeling, almost of light-heartedness, which is at the same time entirely compatible with its use for serious works." The cast type was destroyed in the Parker

*Every type I have designed has been drawn "free-hand."

Building fire of 1908, but the matrices were saved, as they had been placed in the building's safe; and later they passed into the possession of the late Frederick Fairchild Sherman, who purchased the design and whose widow—I think—still retains it. Sherman used the face for the monumental *Catalog of Dutch Paintings* of the Metropolitan Museum.

❧IT WAS THE TERRACE OF
God's house
That she was standing on,—
By God built over the sheer depth
In which Space is begun;
So high, that looking downward

EARLY in 1904 I came across an article on Village Industries, by Sylvester Baxter, in the little magazine *Handicraft* published by the Boston Society of Arts and Crafts. The article mentioned the interesting work of the Arts and Crafts Society at the Village of Hingham, Massachusetts, on Boston Bay. An advertisement of the cabinet work of Vaughan Dennett at Hingham gave me the idea of writing him as to the possibilities of the place for our Village Press. Some weeks later a cordial reply came telling me of a house near his own that was just vacant and could be rented or purchased, and suggesting that I come down and spy out the land.

A modest windfall made the trip possible. Reaching Boston on a Sunday morning, I took an early afternoon train to Hingham—my first visit to a place beside salt water. Hingham was founded in 1635, only a few years after the landing of the Pilgrims some twenty or thirty miles further south, and everything was strange to my mid-western eyes, as even the people themselves were, to many of whom Chicago would have seemed as strange as Hingham was to me.

I asked my way to Dennett's house, which I found without difficulty. On arriving, I used for the first time in my life an old door knocker instead of pushing a button. I was made welcome, and later conducted up the street to the house he had written about. Built in 1790, quaint and interesting in every way, it seemed well adapted to our purposes, as it had a large room in which I could set up our press. The next day I called on the owner at his office in Boston and arranged to rent it. A day or two later Bruce Rogers and his wife accompanied me back to Hingham so that they too might inspect and, I hoped, approve the place, which they did. On returning to Park Ridge I told Mrs. Goudy what I had seen and of the arrangement I had made, only then asking if she were willing to pull up stakes and try the effete East. She replied that she would "go to Timbuctoo if I wanted to go there."

We removed from Park Ridge in March, 1904, to Hingham, Massachusetts, and I took up the grind of earning a living.

CUSHING ITALIC
[Design No. 9]

WHILE in Hingham, Clarence Marder had me draw for him an italic to accompany the Cushing Roman already produced and shown in their specimen. Whether the italic shown in the specimen of today is the one I drew I cannot be sure, so hazy is my memory of the drawings, but I think the type shown there is mine.

For a while commissions from Chicago came along, but in time they dwindled, and Boston had little or no work for a rank Westerner, although one large department store gave me a few commissions. One concern did, however, commission a type face for *The Boston News Letter*, C. W. Barron's financial journal.

*A B C D E F G H I J J K L M
N O P Q R S T U V W X Z
a b c d e f g h i j k l m n o p q r
s t u v w x y z & £ $? ! - ' , : ; .
1 2 3 4 5 6 7 8 9 0*

BARRON'S BOSTON NEWS LETTER
[Design No. 10]

JUST what sort of a letter I did for Barron is not clear in my mind. It must have been a more or less conventional face to replace one that no doubt had been in use for a long time, and was to be set by hand. Linotypes were not as common in 1905 as now. About all I remember of the face is that I turned the drawings over to the manager, whose name I do not now recall, and received my modest honorarium. Nothing further happened regarding this commission until a year or two later, when, after our removal to New York City in 1906, my friend Marder consulted me about the face. Evidently my drawings had been turned over to the American Type Founders Company for making into types and the Company had had Wiebking cut the matrices. At no time since 1906 has any news of the type come to me.

(Readers who may compare the numbering given the types in this review with that of "The Record of Goudy Types," which was printed by the late Dave Gildea for visitors to the celebration of the 35th Anniversary of the Village Press held at Deepdene, July 23, 1938, will note certain differences in the consecutive arrangement; types indicated herein as No. 10 and No. 14 were remembered and added after copy for the earlier list was prepared. Later consideration of the time of the drawing of the types at Hingham makes the present numbering seem more accurate than that in the chronological list in *The Story of the Village Type*.)

ENGRAVERS' ROMAN
[Design No. 11]

WHETHER this type was ever cut or not I am not certain. The face was intended for the use of printers in small towns who were without convenient access to the copperplate engraver, and who wished to print wedding invitations, announcements, etc., in a type that would give more or less the effect of engraved work. Today, I would refuse even to consider such a commission; then, my ideas were not so fixed.

I have said elsewhere "the workman in drawing letters should use the technical limitations of the craft in which he works, to its own advantage. He should not endeavor by trickery to obtain results in one material or method that by right belong to others. Nor should he undertake to master that which in the nature of things is not to be overcome . . . he should not draw in line to imitate the technique of a woodcut, or design a *type* to give the effect of a letter engraved on copper . . ."

I remember making the drawings with Chinese India ink, which I rubbed up from a very fine bit of solid ink from the Columbian Exposition, which had been given me, as it was easier for me to make the very fine strokes and serifs with it than with the Higgins Black ink I ordinarily used. Marder later gave me the original drawings for the face together with the drawings for the Copperplate Gothics, but they were lost in the fire of January, 1939.

COPPERPLATE GOTHICS
[Design No. 12]

I HAD drawn this type for Marder while in Hingham. These drawings, treasured because of their excellence of execution, burned in the fire of 1939. I drew the letters only in the normal weight; from this weight the foundry also made the bold. The type is still shown in the American Type Founders' specimen book and largely used.

A B C D E F G H I J K L M N
O P Q R S T U V W X Y Z &
$ 1 2 3 4 5 6 7 8 9 0 . , ' ; : ! ? -
FWG SAYS: THE OLD
FELLOWS STOLE ALL
OF OUR BEST IDEAS.

CAXTON INITIALS
[Design No. 13]

THESE are a rather clumsy form of Lombardic capitals. At this time I had not given text letters much study and while the forms of these capitals are correct enough, they lack the delicate hair lines which I learned later are an important feature of letters of this kind. Nevertheless, these initials are still shown in the American Type Founders' specimen book.

On one of my visits to the well-known printer John Henry Nash, in San Francisco, I was surprised to learn that he had used them frequently in his printing—I say "surprised" because John Henry never cared much for my types. In a recent little book *About Books*, issued by the University of California Press, the Caxton initials are used on the cover, very effectively stamped in leaf gold; the bold stems giving much of the quality of a mediaeval manuscript letter.

ABCDEFGHIJ
KLMNOPQRS
TUVWXYZ

GLOBE GOTHIC BOLD
[Design No. 14]

This type, drawn at the suggestion of Joseph Phinney, manager of the Boston branch of the American Type Founders Company, followed in the main certain points which he wished brought out. It never had much vogue and is the least satisfactory (to me) of all my types. Phinney paid me a sum that at that time I considered liberal, and I have never been able to free my mind from the suspicion that he wished to help me financially more than he required such a type for his foundry. It was carried in the American Type Founders' specimen book for years, so some fonts must have been sold. Gerry Powell of the A. T. F. insists that it sold in considerable quantities, but I have never come across many pieces of printing showing it in use.

DISTRUST
More Histo
Bold Displa

CASLON REVISED
[Design No. 15]

WHILE I was working in Hingham, Clarence Marder visited me and suggested that he would like to see a type somewhat like Caslon Old Style but without the spottiness which that celebrated face displays. In Caslon Old Style the strong contrast between the over-black stems of the capitals and the light-weight stems in the lower-case—partly due to the height of the capitals—makes a "spotty" page.

I remember that the design I made for Marder showed some departures from the usual rendering of a traditional type face, and this may account for its non-appearance as type. I fear it would not have proved a typographic triumph, even though it was a painstaking, conscientious effort on my part. Yet Marder paid me the *largest* amount for it I had ever received for a type design up to that time.

LIFE in Hingham had become difficult. We made many friends, among them General and Mrs. Osbourne; Mr. and Mrs. Vaughan Dennett, who were largely responsible for our coming there to live; Honorable and Mrs. John D. Long (Ex-Secretary of the Navy); Reverend Charles Park, now pastor of the First Unitarian Church in Boston; Reverend Louis Cornish, and others, but many of the old-timers found it difficult to take such rank Westerners to their bosoms. A commission to do a book for P. K. Foley, the rare-book dealer in Boston, furnished the money to move to New York, where I hoped I might find greater opportunities for earning a living. This was in 1906.

On one of my occasional trips into Boston, my friend the late George French, then editor of *Art in Advertising*, told me he had received a letter from Barnhart Bros. & Spindler, type founders in Chicago, in which they requested him to ask me what I would charge them for a type design. I had, at one time before leaving Chicago for the East, offered Barnhart Bros. & Spindler a type design for which I had the temerity to ask fifteen dollars. The firm kept the design for several months and then returned it with the word that they "didn't know whether it would sell or not." I told French that my idea of price for a type in 1905 was a little different than it was when I was just beginning this work, and to tell Barnhart Bros. & Spindler I wanted $500 for a new design. I have always feared that, since A. E. Barnhart died a week or two later, the shock was too much for him!

While in Hingham we did a book of poems in Village type for Ex-Secretary of the Navy John D. Long, he taking a part of the edition for his own use while we distributed the remainder. I found Long one of the most delightful and kindly men it has ever been my privilege to know.

When we located in New York, I made some new business connections that kept body and soul together, although little or nothing in the way of type orders developed, and then—

"On the night of January 10, 1908, the Village Press, the Village Type, the books and sheets completed and in process of printing, drawings, sketches,

68

everything that I had accumulated in five years, was entirely wiped out by the fire that partially destroyed the Parker Building at 19th Street and Fourth Avenue." Nothing remained for me but to go back to my work as a decorative designer and letter artist and begin anew.

One of my new clients was Frederick Fairchild Sherman, a writer and producer of books; I have mentioned him in my account of the Village type. He formerly had been with Charles Scribner's Sons and for him I did considerable lettering—title pages, etc. He had received an order to prepare the *Catalogue of Dutch Paintings on Exhibition at the Metropolitan Museum of Art*, in connection with the Hudson-Fulton celebration in 1909, and he decided that he would like to use the Village type to print it; but the type itself had of course been destroyed. But the matrices had been saved from the fire—they were the only items saved—and I sold them to him. I drew small capitals for the 16-point size, and had matrices for them, and for the capitals in 22-point, cut by Wiebking, who had cut the original matrices for me in 1903.

MONOTYPE No. 38-e and ITALIC
[Designs No. 16 and No. 17]

SHORTLY after the fire, I was approached by a representative of the printing firm of Redfield, Kendrick and Odell, who were printing the original magazine *Life*, using monotype composition. He had suggested to the Lanston Monotype Machine Company that his firm would like to use a new face for that magazine, and if the Company were willing to undertake the work he would ask me what the cost of such a design would be.

The figure I gave for a roman and italic was ridiculously small, and yet I never even got all of the little that I asked, for the negotiator apparently was afraid to quote to the Company the full amount I was expecting. Anyway, I went ahead with my

ABCDEFGHIJKLM
NOPQRSTUVWXY
Z & Æ Œ : , ' ; : ! ? - fi ff ffi fl ffl
abcdefghijklmnopqrstu
vwxyzæœ£$1234567890

Speaking of earlier types,
Goudy says: The old fellows
stole all of our best ideas:

drawings. At that time I knew absolutely nothing of the Monotype composing machine mechanism, of the die-case and its unit rows, so while my drawings were well enough done, many changes, I fear, had to be made in order to fit my letters to these unit rows, and these changes were made in the Company's drawing room without consultation with me—probably, however, they were as well done as I could have done them. The type finally appeared, but I think long after it was wanted for *Life*.

Just at this time a big department store at 34th Street and Broadway was opened by Gimbel Bros., and the new type was used more or less exclusively by them in their advertising—in fact for a long time it was known as Gimbel, although its official name is 38-E. It has been called, contrary to my wishes, Goudy Old Style and sometimes Goudy Light.

A B C D E F G H I J K L M N O P Q R S T U V W X Y Z & Æ Œ . , ' ; : ! ? - fi ff ffi fl ffl a b c d e f g h i j k l m n o p q r s t u v w x y z æ œ £ $ 1 2 3 4 5 6 7 8 9 0

Speaking of earlier types, Goudy says: The old fellows stole all of our best ideas.

I have been told that a large number of matrices of this face, with its accompanying italic, have been sold, and are still selling. Occasionally used for book work, it is better adapted to advertising text. Munder-Thompson of Baltimore used it in a distinguished format for the story of the new Woolworth Building, for which I did some of the decorative work; the type was selected by the architect of the building. I was proud of my drawings, but the type itself I never have cared for, although it did have, I must admit, a lot to do with putting me on the typographic map.

Orders for commercial designs increased in number and I was able, in 1909, to make my first trip to a foreign shore. On July 5, I embarked, second class, on the old White Star S. S. *Cedric* for London, via Liverpool. After leaving Queenstown, Ireland, something went wrong with the steamer's power plant, and we were landed at Holyhead, North Wales, instead of at Liverpool, and then sent on to London by rail. While I didn't reach Liverpool on that trip, I did see something of North Wales, for which I am glad, as I probably shall never get to make a much-desired walking trip there.

On this first trip abroad I came across nothing especially typographic, except what I saw at the British Museum. William Dana Orcutt had given me a letter to Alfred Pollard, Keeper of the King's Books at the Museum, and he went out of his way to show an unknown typographic upstart many things there which mere tourists would not ordinarily see. In an article I wrote for the *Philobiblon* (Vienna, 1924) I detailed more fully my visit with him. I had also a letter, I think, from Bruce Rogers to Emery Walker, later Sir Emery. He was most kind, inviting me to dinner at "Gatti's" and to his house after dinner, where he showed me his collection of Morris treasures. He gave me his bookplate, printed for him by Morris. This was the first of many visits with him in after years. He gave me a large photogravure portrait of Morris made by him in his own shop, which he inscribed for me and which I cherish today in my own studio.

In 1910 I got together, in my home in Brooklyn, a type cabinet, some quaint types, and a small Golding "Official" hand-lever printing press, with a 9″ x 12″ chase. I gave this press, a few years ago, to my friend Earl Emmons, who has printed a number of charming bits on it. The Village Press was again alive but not particularly active. A little book of *Songs and Verses* by Waller was the first issue from the newly-revived press. This particular book was never regularly published or bound and I still have a few copies in sheet form which I have used for Christmas gifts now and then for friends typographically interested.

NORMAN CAPITALS
[Design No. 18]

ABOUT this time I was doing a great deal of designing and lettering for Norman T. A. Munder, formerly of Munder-Thompson Company in Baltimore.
He had me design a printing-ink catalog for the
George H. Morrill Company of Boston, and the
words "George H. Morrill Company" which I
lettered occurred so frequently in it that I suggested
to Munder that I would have matrices cut for these
letters in 24-point and have type cast. He was agree-
able and the type cast from these matrices was used
in the catalog. Later, I proposed to Munder that I
complete the alphabet of capitals used in the catalog
and have the additional matrices cut. This was done
and the new type called Norman Caps.

I presume Munder still owns these matrices, which
probably are lodged in the vaults of the American
Type Founders, who cast the types for him. Mr.
McArthur of Atlanta, of whom I have previously
spoken, gave me a specimen of the face which he
had printed while he was advertising manager for
Barnhart Bros. & Spindler.

ABCDEFGHIJKLMN
OPQRSTUVWXYZA

SEE THE QUICK
BROWN FOX JUMP

MCMXI

Up to this point the reconstruction of these details has been hard. Since in January 1908 the records of types already made, and most of the correspondence relating to them, had been destroyed, I have had to glean my facts from meager printed matter, augmented by personal recollections which, while clear —for I have a good memory—are not, of course, infallible. But now (1911) I reach a time when my records are more complete, and when the typographic tide turns: I abandon my "amateur" standing and my life work as a professional type designer really begins.

KENNERLEY OLD STYLE
[Design No. 19]

Mitchell Kennerley, a New York publisher, showed me one day early in 1911 a "dummy" (which I still have) prepared for him by Alvin Langdon Coburn, an English photographer, of "The Door in the Wall," by H. G. Wells with photographic illustrations in photogravure made for it by Coburn, who proposed also to make and print the illustrations which, in the book, would be "tipped in." Kennerley asked me if I cared to plan the arrangement of the book and make whatever decorative features I thought it might require. Of course, I was delighted with such an interesting commission.

The size of Coburn's prints really set the key for its size and shape (11 x 13½"), and I decided to have a couple of trial pages of Wells' copy set in 18-point Caslon Old Face, 38 ems measure. My layout, showing size of page, with position of type and margins indicated, I sent to my friend Munder, in Baltimore. In a few days press proofs of my layout, beautifully printed on handmade paper were received. As I studied them, a feeling of disappointment came over me. Something didn't "click": what was it? I took the pages to Kennerley and told him of my dissatisfaction; naturally he asked what other type would please me more. I replied that I had already gone carefully through specimens for types that seemed suitable and that Caslon was the best I could find. Whereupon he asked "what was wrong with Caslon?" I had by this time decided that the pages presented a spotty appearance, largely due to the strong contrast in color between the capitals and the lower-case, and partly due to the wide fitting of the letters themselves, making it impossible to present each word as a compact unit, which I felt was desirable, for only if each word is a compact unit can close spacing between words be used.

His next question "What shall we do now?" brought from me a suggestion (to which I hardly expected a favorable reply)—"Why not make a new type for the book?" This solution, he feared, would be too expensive, but as he hadn't turned it down completely, I went on to explain that since he intended to pay me for making the book, I would—if he would advance something on account monthly—design a type, have matrices cut and type cast by my friend Wiebking in Chicago, and then, after the book itself was printed, I would attempt to sell fonts of the type to *discriminating* printers, hoping thus to recoup in part at least the expense of procuring it. This suggestion met his approval, but neither he nor I at that time could foresee the more or less popular acceptance of the new letter when it was later offered for sale to printers.

On one of his periodic trips to England Kennerley had brought me a book from Quaritch's—it was *A Century of Typography at the Oxford University Press* by Horace Hart, printer to the Press. It showed the Fell types, which Bishop Fell had imported about 1671 for use at the Press, and I used the great canon size shown in that book as a *basis* for my new type. I had drawn maybe a dozen letters when I noticed a movement in my own type drawings not shown by the specimen types in Hart's book; I was working free-hand and I had gradually drawn away from my exemplar and pursued a line of my own; I went back over the letters already drawn, and brought them into harmony as to details with those that followed more completely my own conception of a new face. My drawings, as I remember them, were about one inch high and very carefully executed—in those days I could do such work in ink very well. The actual drawings were later turned over to Caslon's in London, who purchased the English and Continental rights to the design in 1913.

Stanley Morison, the distinguished writer on typographic matters, says that "Kennerley is an original face, that is to say, its essential characteristics are not drawn from existing sources, at least as far as the Roman is concerned." My own description of the face in *Typographica No. 2*, June, 1912, was: "Kennerley Old Style is a book letter with strong serifs, firm hairlines, and makes a solid, compact page." Of it Mitchell Kennerley, for whom it is named,

A B C D E F G H I J K L M N O P
Q R S T U V W X Y Z & Æ Œ ℭ]
a b c d e f g h i j k l m n o p q r s t u v w x y z
æ œ fi ff ffi fl ffl ct st . , ' ; : ! ? - $ 1 2 3 4 5 6 7 8 9 0

Speaking of earlier types,
Goudy says: The old fellows
stole all of our best ideas.

said: "The new face was flexible. Its close-fitting quality made it possible to space words closely without loss of legibility."

I intended at first to cut the design in 16-point only, the size I had planned to use for the Wells book, but I decided that as I was going in debt for one size I might as well "be hung for a sheep as for a lamb"—and I ordered the 12-point size also. Some time later, finding I needed an intermediate size for a book for the National Biscuit Company, I went to Chicago and superintended the cutting and casting of the 14-point size. To meet a deadline as to production, Wiebking, dubious at first, finally consented to attempt a typographic *tour de force*. As each matrix was engraved, it was fitted and sent direct to the casters without waiting until all of the 103 characters were engraved, and within *ten* working days about 600 lbs. of type were shipped to J. J. Little & Ives, New York City, who were to print the book for the National Biscuit Company. This commission gave me an opportunity to renew my acquaintance with Earl Babst, president of the Biscuit Company, whom I had known as a young attorney in Detroit when I was cashier for the farm paper there in 1897-9.

Kennerley type at this writing is over thirty years old, and still sells. In 1920 I made an arrangement with the Lanston Monotype Machine Company giving it the sole reproduction rights in this country, but that did not prevent its misappropriation by a type foundry and a composing-machine company, each renaming it for its own purposes, and selling types and matrices without any return to me. Caslon in London owns the English and Continental rights.

This is the true story of a type which "came about in a most natural and casual way." I have often been amused by imaginary accounts of its provenance by ignorant critics.

After the Monotype Company had made their reproduction of Kennerley—which they did with fidelity to my design, even going so far as to provide a mechanical equipment that would enable the monotype owner to use the composition sizes without changing the "sets" of the type as I furnished it —they added some "Kennerley Open Caps" by cutting a white line through each as shown below. For many places where an initial was needed, the open caps provided a letter which was large enough without being too black.

[Design No. 19A]

A B C D E F
GHIJKLM
TUV&12

FORUM TITLE
[Design No. 20]

WHILE working on my Wells book layout, I felt it
would be well to have a heading letter for the titles
of the different stories and for use on the title-page.
I remembered that when in Rome with my wife in
1910 I had been struck with the inscriptional letters
on the Trajan Column, on the Arch of Titus in the
Roman Forum, and on stray marble slabs. From one
of these slabs I had gotten an interesting rubbing of
three or four beautiful capitals, which suggested to
me a basis for my new heading letter. With these
rubbings to suggest the weight of stems, movement,
etc., I began the drawings, not trying, however, to
copy or imitate them, or in fact *any* particular inscriptional letter, but simply to get into my drawings something of the feeling of the monumental
characters evolved by the stone-cutters of ancient
Rome. It was to be an alphabet of capitals only, for
lower-case letters didn't come into existence for several hundred years after Roman times. In a sense,
therefore, Forum Title is a composite letter; it is,

A B C D E F G H I J K L M N
O P Q R S T U V W X Y Z &
1 2 3 4 5 6 7 8 9 0 ′ . ,

FWG SAYS ′ THE OLD FELLOWS
STOLE ALL OF OUR BEST IDEAS

however, original in design. It was not copied from any existing inscription: while it does indeed incorporate a number of features common to all the classic lapidary forms of the first centuries of the Christian Era, no inscription exists that will exactly suggest the face as finally cut in type.

Stanley Morison said of Forum Title that "it is a very handsome letter," and Bruce Rogers, in his article on the "Progress of Modern Printing in the United States" for the *London Times* Printing Number in 1912, was kind enough to say that "[Goudy] has already produced one or two fonts distinguished by their successful rendering of classic feeling. Of these the capitals known as 'Forum' are the most beautiful, and have been widely used and imitated." Both the Kennerley and Forum drawings were made within one week's time.

That Forum is a patented face did not deter one type founder from putting out a copy under a different name. When Forum was first offered to printers generally I was amused when a man walked into my office on Madison Avenue one morning and asked "is this the place that sells Forum type?" I said it was, and showed him a specimen sheet of the sizes I could furnish. He picked out several fonts and asked to have them wrapped up. The bill amounted to something like thirty dollars, and as he didn't have a particularly prosperous look I was surprised when he produced a roll of bills at least two inches in diameter tied with string, from which he handed me the amount of my bill. I asked if he had a card, so I could keep a record of the transaction, and he handed me one of cheap pasted circus bristol, set in five or six types of the 80's. I have often wondered what he wanted my type for, but alas! I have never seen him since.

The Lanston Monotype Company has the sole reproduction rights in this country and the Caslons in London own the English and Continental rights to the face. The face sold well and is still selling after thirty-odd years on the market.

FREDICSHAMNGT
pack my box with five
dzn lqur jgs 1234567
890 Qu& æ œ ct fl ffi
YQULVKJPZBWX,-

SHERMAN
[Design No. 21]

SHERMAN
[Design No. 21]

FREDERICK SHERMAN, of whom I have spoken earlier, was doing some publishing and he decided he would like an exclusive type for his own use. He already had my Village type. I felt that a new type for him should present a marked difference from that face in character. The letter I made for him is one of my disappointments. The drawings were really beautiful, but the type as cut in 14-point proved difficult to use. I had at that time, due to inexperience, concluded that "close fitting" of a type was a *sine qua non*, and in the Sherman type I went to extremes.

For a trial showing of the new face Sherman had chosen Bliss Carman's *A Painter's Holiday* and Bertha set up a couple of facing pages in the new type, from which I pulled some trial proofs to show the quality of impression I wanted; and then sent all the type to Munder for printing. The book was to be on an Italian hand-made paper, which Sherman had imported. My proofs were carefully printed on *dampened* stock, which permitted a solid black impression with each letter clean and distinct, but Munder endeavored to get the same effect my proof showed by excess ink on dry paper, with the result that many letters practically ran into each other. Where the type now is I do not know, as Sherman and I quarrelled later over other business matters and I never saw him again.

[See specimen reproduction on opposite page]

GOUDY LANSTON
[Design No. 22]

THIS face has had a number of names. In 1912
Robert Hewitt of Ardsley, New York, a great Lincoln enthusiast, commissioned the late Frederic
Trevor Hill, a prominent Wall Street attorney and a
writer who specialized in articles about Lincoln, to
write a book on "Lincoln as a Lawyer." Hill's copy
was turned over to me to plan the book, which was
to be unlike any other. Not only was I to design a
new type for it, but Hewitt had commissioned
Mowbray Clarke, the sculptor, to make a plaque for
it, two hundred copies to be struck in bronze (ten in
silver, and one in gold) in size 1¾ x 2¾ inches. This
plaque bore on one face a profile bust of Lincoln,
and on the reverse a standing female figure of
"Justice," with a sword held crosswise by each hand.
This plaque was to be mounted opposite the title
page, and, just below it, was to be mounted a thin

ABCDEFGHIJKLMNOP
QRSTUVWXYZ&.,';:!?~
abcdefghijklmnopqrstuvwx
yzfiffffiflffl&æœ$1234567890

Speaking of earlier types,
Goudy says: The old fellows
stole all of our best ideas.

veneer about ¾ inch wide by 3 or 4 inches long cut from the edge of a board from the actual flooring of Lincoln's office in Springfield.

Whether this page would ever have worked out I do not know, as Hewitt died suddenly, though not before the setting of the pages for the book had been completed. His death left me with the type composition done, the type cut and cast in the 16-point size; but unfortunately I was in no position to carry out the book as we had planned it. Hill had been paid for his work and had little further interest in it, so the proofs and copy were laid aside. I named the type "Goudy Old Style" and put it on the market to try to recover my expense of cutting, etc. Quite recently I was pleased to find Hill's copy, my suggested layout, and proofs of the text of the book, among my papers.

In *Typographica No. 2*, 1912, I said of the type that "it is a sturdy letter free from affectation or caprice. . . . Mr. Goudy believes that in this new letter he has rediscovered a principle in spacing individual letters used by letter founders before the 16th century, but not since, a principle to which the harmonious quality of a page of Jenson is largely due. Each letter stands on solid serifs of unusual shape which are so planned as to make each letter form conterminous with the type body, while maintaining sufficient white space to set each letter off from its neighbor without destroying the unity of the word formed by its separate characters, thus permitting close spacing and avoiding looseness of composition." If I had done the same thing with the "Sherman" type (No. 21), it might have proved less disappointing. Goudy Old Style was cut in one size only.

Two or three years later, when I made a new face for the American Type Founders Company, I released the name "Goudy Old Style" for this new face to that Foundry, at the request of Robert Nelson, the president, as he thought the name most suitable for the new design. I thereupon renamed my own letter "Goudy Antique." Many years later, when Mr. Best of the Lanston Monotype Company wished to put the face on the machine, he asked permission to name their production of it "Goudy Lanston," in honor of Tolbert Lanston, the inventor of that famous composing machine. Caslon and Company of London own the English rights and they ruined the face (in my estimation) by putting it on standard line, and shortening the descenders to fit; also adding insult to injury by calling it "Ratdolt." It does not resemble Ratdolt's famous letter in any particular. The Caslons cut matrices and sent them to this country—an act contrary to the customary ethics, since the Caslons owned the English rights only—giving Hart, Schaffner & Marx the "exclusive" right to the face. To this I protested, but took no other action against such a breach of rights. I still own the design.

Homep Homep Ho
poem pope mop
mmmmmm oooooo
eeeeeeeeeeee ppppp

GOUDY ROMAN [Design No. 23]

GOUDY ROMAN
[Design No. 23]

LUNCHING one day with Louis H. Orr of the Bartlett Press, at the New York Advertising Club, then located on 24th Street near Madison Avenue, he asked me what an exclusive type for his Company would cost. I probably told him it would depend on the number of sizes he might want, and just what arrangement was made I do not remember; but anyway he said to "go ahead." I already had arranged with Caslon's to engrave matrices and cast type for me, as they were then doing that work for the types they had purchased from me, and I suggested to Orr that, as I was planning to go abroad, probably in June, I would make drawings for him; and if they pleased him, I would take them along and have punches cut by the Caslons.

The drawings were finished in due time and submitted to Orr. I made my steamer reservation, but I didn't hear definitely from Orr until the morning of the day I was to sail. About an hour before sailing time I succeeded in getting a check on account from the firm. Clarence Marder of the American Type Founders Company had, in the meantime, arranged to go with me and I had the pleasure of his company on my visit to Sidney Caslon, managing director of H. W. Caslon & Company who, in a few minutes, agreed to take some four or five new designs from me. This impressed Clarence so much that on our return to New York he reported our visit to Caslon's to Robert Nelson, President of American Type Founders, and suggested that the Company commission a type from me. The result of his suggestion appears later.

While Clarence and I were in London, rumblings of war began to be felt, and when Sidney Caslon wished to make me a payment, he personally had to go to the British Treasury for permission to let the amount go out of England. He gave me a first and second bill of exchange, one to keep and one to mail to my own address in America. The day following my arrival home I received the bill I had mailed in London—it had come over on the *same* steamer with me, so in case of shipwreck both it and the one I had with me would have been lost!

Owing to the talk of war, Caslon's would not accept my order to engrave the Orr type and I brought the drawings back with me. I returned to Bartlett-Orr the amount of their preliminary payment, as they had cooled somewhat toward the idea. The drawings lay around for some time, and then Mr. Murray of Barnhart Bros. & Spindler said he would cut some trials for me. I made a few revisions and sent them to him. The matrices he cut were beautifully engraved, very deep and sharp, but the design disappointed me and I did nothing with it at that time. Later, when I was engraving matrices myself, I revamped the design, renaming the face "Goudy Roman." I have in my desk three or four pieces of type cast in the B. B. & S. matrices. Of the face nothing remains but these and a proof, here reproduced, showing the B. B. & S. cutting. This might have been a pleasant, but I fear not a very distinguished, type.

[See specimen reproduction on page 88]

KLAXON
[Design No. 24]

The same year (1914) in which I designed the "Goudy Roman," the advertising manager for Lovell, McConnell & Company of Newark, New Jersey, manufacturers of the famous Klaxon Auto Warning Signal, asked me to design a letter for their advertising. I had been working on a design intended tentatively for the Curtis Publishing Company, who paid me for my sketches, but who for some reason or other decided not to go on with the project. I showed these drawings to the president of Lovell, McConnell and he liked them. I finished the drawings and sent them out to Wiebking to engrave matrices. He cut three sizes, but whether he also cast the type I am not now certain. I had the matrices in my possession for a number of years and they were lost in the 1939 fire. Klaxon products were later taken over by General Motors and this design evidently was overlooked, as the Klaxon advertising was merged into that of the larger company. The specimen shown here has been photographed from an advertisement, as no type remains. It was not a fine type, although it did present some unusual details of handling. It was not a bad publicity letter.

A WARNING SIGNAL must not only waves on the drum of the ear, but it mind behind the ear and cause volitional signal should carry its alarm notice over the least one block, to even a deaf or slow-moving the wind and other noise of the street.

GOUDY OLD STYLE
[Design No. 25]

As I have previously said, Clarence Marder had
suggested to Mr. Nelson, president of the American
Type Founders Company, that he ought to commission a type from me for the Company. On the occasion of one of my frequent visits to the Company,
then located in Jersey City, Marder said Nelson
would like to see me. I had never met him in person,
but on going into his office I found him very pleasant and affable. He said that Clarence had been telling him of our London experiences and particularly
of our visit with the Caslons. He went on to say that
I "was beginning to found a type school more or
less my own, and would I consider making a design

ABCDEFGHIJKLMN
OPQRSTUVWXYZ&
ABCDEFGHIJKLMNOPQRS
TUVWXYZ&fi ff ffi fl ffl .,';:!?-
abcdefghijklmnopqrst
uvwxyz$1234567890

Speaking of earlier types,
Goudy says: The old fellows
stole all of our best ideas.

for him?" I said I would be glad to, *if* I could do just what I thought best as to design without interference by the foundry's drawing room. He replied that that was "exactly what he wanted."

I began my drawings; I had at some time or other copied a few letters of classic form from a portrait painting—I have always said "by Hans Holbein," but later search has never brought these particular pattern letters to light. Anyway, I decided that I would attempt to complete an alphabet of capitals along the lines of the letters I had copied. Then came the difficult task of designing a lower-case in perfect harmony with classic capitals which harked back to a period some hundreds of years earlier.

My troubles began. The first proofs of my design from the foundry showed differences from my drawings. I immediately took the matter up with Nelson and reminded him of his promise that my design would be followed exactly. He expressed surprise that it had not been so followed, but I soon convinced him that I was right, and he immediately gave orders that no changes should be made unless, after submission to me, I approved them; and also that the already changed characters should be replaced by others following my drawings exactly. The face, as finally produced, was, I felt, *almost* as great an innovation in type as my Kennerley. It immediately "took" and large quantities have been sold; and it is still selling.

I am almost satisfied that the design is a good one, marred only by the short descenders which I allowed the American Type Founders to inveigle me into giving p, q, g, j, and y—though only under protest.

On a visit to the American Type Founders some years ago by members of the American Institute of Graphic Arts, they were accompanied through the different departments by the Librarian, the late Henry T. Bullen, who, stopping at one of the big automatic casters, which was pouring out an endless stream of glistening types, remarked that the types being cast were the latest from a design by one of the Institute's own members. He went on to say: "Here is where Goudy goes down to posterity, while the American Type Founders Company goes down to prosperity." I fear he was too optimistic on both counts.

From the parent design the American Type Founders Company developed Goudy Bold, Extra Bold and Italics, to form a combination called the "Goudy Family" but with which I had absolutely no part; nor did I ever receive any compensation for this use of my name. Also, by enlarging the small capitals to a height almost that of the type body—thereby increasing the weight of the letters—a new character was developed which was named "Goudy Title." To permit a larger face without kern, the "Q" was redesigned at the foundry to a form which irritates me mightily.

GOUDY OLD STYLE ITALIC
[Design No. 26]

OF COURSE an italic was needed for the roman, and I didn't know just what kind to draw. Up to this time I had attempted only two other italic types, so a good many preliminary sketches were made (for my own satisfaction) before seriously beginning one for Goudy Old Style. I studied many of the older italics and came to the conclusion that except for equivalent weight and general harmony with the roman, there was no rule to be followed for the italic, even in the matter of inclination—notwithstanding Douglas McMurtrie's dictum that the degree of inclination should be 17 per cent. I found that some of the outstanding italics of the sixteenth century had little or no inclination and yet preserved

A B C D E F G G H I J J K L M N O P Q R S T T U V W X Y Y Z & fi ff ffi fl ffl ct Qu a b c d e f g h i j k l m n o p q r s t u v w x y z . , ' ; : ! ? - $ 1 2 3 4 5 6 7 8 9 0

Speaking of earlier types, Goudy says: The old fellows stole all of our best ideas.

their italic character. Eleven years after I had drawn Goudy Old Style Italic, Stanley Morison said: "The quality of slope is no true test of an italic."

I found, too, that at the time of England's early printer, John Daye, circa 1578, one italic might be used satisfactorily with several romans, so long as lining, height of forms, and harmony as to weight with the roman with which it was used were considered.

Taking the Aldine italic as a starting point for my new font I began my work, and succeeded in producing an original letter which, I believe, constituted the first distinctive italic in modern times. It has been praised by Henry L. Bullen and Stanley Morison, and has been used for some important items by Bruce Rogers and Francis Meynell.

I had found that the principal feature of a good italic was a certain informality, as well as a peculiar elegance and freedom in construction. Henry Bullen said "this distinctive and charming italic face will give the printed page the touch of individuality which the wide-awake printer esteems."

GOUDY CURSIVE
[Design No. 27]

CLARENCE MARDER suggested that the italic I made
to accompany the Goudy Old Style roman might
have an added utility if I added some characters to
give it a still greater appearance of freedom and informality, and also give it something of the quality
of hand-lettering. I worked out my own interpreta-
tion of early Roman cursive writing, and, with the
italic as a foundation, drew a number of capital and
lower-case forms, logotypes, flourishes, etc., in the
spirit of the italic already made, and which I hoped
would, if used with discrimination, brighten an
otherwise more commonplace showing.

A B C D E F G H I J K L M
N O P Q R S T U V W X Y Z &
a b c d e f g h i j k l m n o p q r s t u v w x y z
A J K N R Qu Qu Th e g k m
n r v w x Qu ct st ſs . , ' ' ; : ! ? -
~ ~ $ 1 2 3 4 5 6 7 8 9 0 ~ ~
Speaking of earlier types, Goudy says:
The old fellows stole all of our best ideas.

BOOKLET OLD STYLE
[Design No. 28]

ABOUT this time I drew for the American Type
Founders Company a letter simple in construction,
plain and unobtrusive, as one of the types called for
by an arrangement I had just made with the company to design exclusively for it. Some time later
when I was shown proofs of the face (which did not
seem terribly distinctive) I gave it the name "Booklet Old Style" after my first press in Chicago in 1895.
I do not think the company ever gave the letter any
special advertising. I have proofs of it as first cut,
but I do not recall ever seeing it displayed in the
company's specimen books.

One of the that all attempt
lasting lesson for graft pers
bright see these song notes
stone shone those nests co
the seventh regiment rollin
SHE SEES HOMES SHE
COMMON SENSE HAS

NATIONAL OLD STYLE
[Design No. 29]

CLARENCE MARDER asked me later that same year whether I could use the lettering I had done for the National Biscuit Company in 1901 or 1902 and make a type approximating it in character. I called his attention to the fact that the lettering he referred to consisted of capitals only, and while it would be easy enough to make a type of those, it would be more difficult to make a lower-case which would not be rather freakish to go with them.

However, I went ahead with the design, adding a lower-case in harmony with the capitals, and it is shown in the specimens of the company. I see it occasionally in printing; one use of it, I recall, is on the cover and title page of *Graphic Arts* issued by

A B C D E F G H I J K L M N
O P Q R S T U V W X Y Z &
a b c d e f g h i j k l m n o p q r s
t u v w x y z fi ff fl ffi ffl .,;':!?-$
1 2 3 4 5 6 7 8 9 0

Speaking of earlier types, Goudy says:
The old fellows stole all of our best ideas.

the Encyclopaedia Britannica for a selection of articles from its 14th edition. It has also been used for captions for movies, owing to its strong but even color. As a display letter it probably compares favorably with many others we could do without.

GOUDYTYPE
[Design No. 30]

THIS letter is one of those drawn as a result of my connection with the American Type Founders Company. I was pleased with it at the time of its making, for I felt it presented a liveliness of handling not hitherto expressed in type. It really did that very thing, but that in itself was not enough to make it a good type. At this time I was beginning to find myself; but as yet neither my studies nor my conclusions had given me the sureness and authoritative grasp of type problems I hope I command today; and I fear I allowed matters of mere technique to influence me —often mistaking excellence in the handling of details for excellence of design.

The foundry made a four-page specimen of Goudytype, showing it in thirteen sizes, and calling it "an original design." One feature of the face was the introduction of roman "swash" capitals among the usual capital forms, and printers frequently inter-

A B C D E F G H I J K L
M N O P Q R S T U V W
X Y Z a b c d e f g h i j k l m
n o p q r s t u v w x y z $ &
. : ; , - ! ? ' 1 2 3 4 5 6 7 8 9 0

polated these freakish letters into the middle of words set in capitals, where they certainly did not belong. Their occasional use might be desirable as initial letters of words in lines where a touch of quaintness is required, and that is where I intended they should be used.

In the summer of 1942, while in Los Angeles, I was shown some proofs of the face by a printer there, and I had really to study them a bit before I could say what type it was: so completely had it escaped my memory.

ADVERTISERS' ROMAN
[Design No. 31]

READERS of these lines will have to accept my word for it that drawings for this type were made, for nothing remains to substantiate my statement except the memorandum in *The Story of The Village Type* issued in 1933, at a time when the drawings were still intact. Why nothing was done to produce the design I cannot now remember. Probably I wished to make some revisions and just didn't get around to the work. Maybe it's just as well that the drawings burned in 1939, for I don't think they were any too good!

AN UNNAMED DESIGN

WHILE in Forest Hills Gardens I designed this type face, and in an attempt better to judge its effect I had zinc etchings made of the drawings, and a number of proofs pulled from them. From the proofs I cut individual letters which I pasted up in words to give the effect of type. Evidently the effect was not as good as I had hoped it would be and the drawings were laid aside. I recall that on the occasion of a visit to my home by Frank Berry, afterwards Vice-President of the A.T.F., I showed them to him. He seemed to think they offered a basis for a type, but was not very enthusiastic over them. Every now and then I would come across these proofs and I would try to figure out just what was wrong with the design, but decided finally that fundamentally it just wasn't good.

I had thought that the drawings burned in 1939, but discovered otherwise when in December, 1943, I sent my typographic library and certain materials

PCK MY BX WITH
FV DZN JUGS LQR
quick brown fog day U
12 & l m j v z s fi x
BARDOE peath᷄ g

used in my typographic work to the Library of Congress in Washington. While packing items for shipment, the original drawings for No. 31A turned up, and are here reproduced.

KENNERLEY ITALIC
[Design No. 32]

I CANNOT imagine just why I put off for seven years the making of an italic to accompany Kennerley Old Style. The sales of Kennerley were good and certainly an italic was called for. Probably I was timid about attempting another italic. Maybe I feared that I had "shot my bolt" when I made Goudy Old Style Italic. However, I began the drawings, again looking to the Fell italic for inspiration as I had to the Fell roman for Kennerley Old Style, and just as I had done for the roman I soon discarded my exemplar and took my own path, producing an italic that immediately took its place among "the best sellers." Of it Stanley Morison said: "the pretty italic is obviously not without affinity to the famous prototype of Aldus (1501)." It is still used, and only recently appropriated without permission and distributed under a different though reminiscent name. The Monotype Company owns the rights of reproduction for the United States—the design itself is still my property.

A B C D E F G H I J K L M N O

P Q R S T U V W X Y Z & Æ Œ

a b c d e f g h i j k l m n o p q r s t u v w x y z

æ œ fi ff ffi fl ffl . , ' ; : ! ? - $ 1 2 3 4 5 6 7 8 9 0

CLOISTER INITIALS
[Design No. 32A]

"Wad" Parker of the American Type Founders Company one day called my attention to the large initial "A" which I had used in my book *The Alphabet*, just published by Mitchell Kennerley, and asked me if I would complete for the A.T.F. the remaining letters of the alphabet in the same spirit and character. This I did, and I produced what he was pleased to say "were the best G— d—d initials ever made." Maybe he was a little strong both as to sentiment and appreciation, but Cloister initials have had a long and useful life and are still extensively used and *copied*. I include them in this account of my types not because they are "types" in the usual sense, but because the foundry actually engraved matrices from my drawings and *cast* the initials as type in a type mould.

In the *Record of Goudy Types* Cloister initials are inaccurately numbered "93." They are properly placed here, but too late to be given the proper consecutive number without renumbering all of the designs following them. In *The Story of The Village Type* Cloister initials were mentioned as designed in 1916, which is incorrect, since *The Alphabet* was not published until 1918.

HADRIANO TITLE
[Design No. 33]

In July, 1910, while Bertha and I were in Paris, we
visited the Louvre. One day while strolling through
a room devoted to inscribed marbles and monu-
ments of the first centuries A.D., we came across a
tablet about four and a half by eight feet in size,
inscribed with a number of lines of capital letters in
several sizes. I caught the word "Hadriano," and
asking Bertha to watch for a guard, I tore a leaf out
of my notebook and made a rubbing of three letters
which I thought were characteristic. The letters were
P, E, and R, and I still have the rubbing.

One evening in 1918 while going through some
papers I came across this rubbing and the thought
came to me that I might add the other twenty-three
letters of the alphabet and from them make a new
type conceived in the same spirit as the original inscription.

By eleven o'clock that Sunday night I had traced

ABCDEFGHIJKLMN
OPQRSTUVWXYZ.·,
1234567890&

FWG SÁYS: THE OLD
FELLOWS STOLE ÁLL

the three letters (correcting only the broken edges) and added what I conceived to be letters that might accompany them harmoniously. I made absolutely no change in the actual weight or form of the three letters which I had rubbed, and in a day or two sent the drawings for the alphabet to Wiebking in Chicago who cut matrices for the 24-point size and cast some fonts for me.

I did not order a large number of fonts cast, as I did not imagine printers would accept such an innovation; but to my surprise I had to re-order frequently to keep up with an unexpected demand for the type. In 1927, after I had begun cutting matrices and casting types at my own "Village Letter Foundery," I made patterns and cut matrices for sizes twelve to thirty-six point.

The University of California Press has used Hadriano in the printing of its diplomas for several years, setting in it some 4000 names of graduates each year. And only recently Bruce Rogers has used the face to print "The Atlantic Charter," with a heading in Forum—using both faces much better than I could have done myself. The Monotype Company owns the reproduction rights.

GOUDY OPEN
[Design No. 34]

THE idea for this type was suggested by the caption of a French engraving used as a frontispiece to Alfred Pollard's *Fine Books*. I say "the idea," because the actual form of my letters followed those of the engraving only in spirit and not in facsimile. As I worked I developed a quality in the forms of the letters which differed from anything I hitherto had produced. The letter forms had something of a "modern" look; but in an attempt to give a quality of interest and legibility which the "modern" types of Bodoni lacked, I bravely increased (unlike Bodoni and his school) the weight of the hairlines, bracketed the serifs slightly, and carried my curves more generously toward the stems. In this way I gave strength to the letters constructively and avoided the appearance in print of a "mere jumble of heavy lines fretted here and there with greyness," a quality in Bodoni's types which requires constant readjustment of eye focus and constitutes the essential fault of his letter.

A B C D E F G H I J K L M
N O P Q R S T U V W X Y
Z & . , ' ; : ! ? - fi ff fl ffi ffl
a b c d e f g h i j k l m n o p q r s
t u v w x y z 1 2 3 4 5 6 7 8 9 0

GOUDY MODERN
[Design No. 35]

WHEN I had before me the first proofs of my Goudy Open, I put a proof of one of the larger point sizes on my drawing board and filled in the "white line" solidly in ink. I decided that with a minimum of trouble I could thus procure another type which would complement the Open already made, and, as I liked the effect of the solid letter, I ordered the cutting of this second type also, calling it Goudy Modern.

Goudy Modern had its first showing in the quarterly magazine *Ars Typographica*, Vol. I, No. 2, which the late Hal Marchbanks and I started in the Spring of 1918. The magazine was spoken of highly by every one for whom it was *not* specifically intended. I figured that the material we wanted to present, "although familiar to most collectors and

A B C D E F G H I J K L M
N O P Q R S T U V W X Y
Z & . , ' ; : ! ? - fi ff fl ffi ffl
a b c d e f g h i j k l m n o p q r s
t u v w x y z 1 2 3 4 5 6 7 8 9 0

Speaking of earlier types, Goudy says:
The old fellows stole all of our best ideas.

bibliophiles, would interest the printer disinclined to research, as it would furnish cut-and-dried bits of typographic lore and information not otherwise easily available to him. To the Editor's surprise (and chagrin) printers, for whom the publication was planned, cared for it not a damn, and librarians, book collectors, advertising typographers and other printing laymen, most of whom already had the contents of the magazine in some form or other in their own libraries, bought it." Only a few printers cared for it, even as a specimen of beautiful printing —which it was. In this magazine Goudy Modern had its first showing and description.

Stanley Morison, in one number of *The Fleuron*, says that "it is strikingly handsome in mass . . . The type reads easily, and in spite of the fact that it is, on the whole, a condensed fount, the weight is so nicely judged and the thicks and thins so cleverly adjusted that the effect is rather generous and open.'

This face was sold to the English Monotype Company for England and its Colonies. Caslon's, after seeing it in *Ars Typographica*, arranged with the English Monotype Company to issue the face, and the Company agreed to cut a duplicate set of punches, one set for Caslon's use. Their cutting was good but a little too precise, and the face thereby lost that intangible quality of freedom, that indescribable something which the designer would give to the face were he cutting his own punches.

The name "Modern" is perhaps unfortunate, since the face really is not a true "modern" letter, although based on one. It presents here and there some "old-style" tendencies.

COLLIER OLD STYLE
[Design No. 36]

In the Spring of 1919 I was invited by Allan Collier of Proctor & Collier, advertising agency, to address a printer's organization in Cincinnati. At the luncheon given me, he asked what it might cost for his concern to have its own exclusive type. We talked over the number of sizes that he needed and other details of its use, including its probable cost. A few days later, on my return home, I received his letter authorizing me to make a design for their use. The agency had its own printing plant.

On my first visit to London in 1909 I had purchased at the South Kensington Museum several sheets of photographs of old types. Among them was one of a type page printed at Basle by Palma Isingrin in 1534. One word of this page contained a lower-case "d" which exhibited a peculiar serif on the ascender—due, I imagine, to damage—but the changed shape gave me an idea for the serifs which I used in the other letters with ascenders in the design I was making for Mr. Collier.

When I had finished my drawings, and before submitting them to Collier, I sent them to Wiebking and had the 16-point size cut. When a proof of this was ready Collier came to New York on one of his frequent trips and I then showed the proof to him. He was very much pleased and urged me to get the other sizes cut as rapidly as possible. Louis Braverman had by this time joined the agency as printer, the Press occupying a new building just erected by the company—one of the finest printing-office buildings I ever saw. It presented much of the feeling of the Plantin Press at Antwerp and I think Collier had that celebrated press in mind while building. At one time Braverman prepared, for insertion in a special number of *The American Printer*, a page showing the "Collier Old Style," which seemed to me to give a quality akin to that given by William Morris's Golden type without, however, imitating that famous letter.

Collier's untimely death was a loss to good advertising, good typography, and to mankind. His sterling honesty and sincerity made it a pleasure to work for him, and I greatly deplore the loss of a genuine friend. The world, to me, seems vastly poorer without him.

All of the drawings except one sheet showing the letters "LRJUGS lqurjgs&" were burned in 1939. I recut the ampersand I had made for the Collier font, and used it in my article on "Ands and Ampersands" printed in the Typophile *Diggings from Many Ampersandhogs*, for which book I drew and engraved over sixty "short ands."

ABCDEFGH I JKLMNO
PQRSTUVWXYZabcd
efghijklmnopqrstuvw
xyz&$,;:.-'!?1234567890

GOUDY MODERN ITALIC
[Design No. 37]

ALTHOUGH Goudy Open preceded Goudy Modern
in cutting, Goudy Modern Italic drawings were made
before cutting the Open Italic. It was a difficult
letter to design, yet Stanley Morison in *The Fleuron*
says "the italic, though possibly more original* in
design than the roman, is consistently conservative
in spirit." The face is identical with the Open Italic
except that it presents a solid face instead of a white
line in its stems. Caslon's bought the English rights,
and for it the English Monotype Company cut
punches. The American Monotype Company owns
the reproduction rights; the design itself is my
property.

A B C D E F G H I J K L M N

O P Q R S T U V W X Y Z &

abcdefghijklmnopqrstuvwxyz

fiff ffi fl ffl 1234567890 .,';:!?-

Speaking of earlier types, Goudy says:

The old fellows stole all of our best ideas.

*By way of reply to Mr. Morison, I may say that the
roman was definitely based on an *existing* exemplar, but the
italic had no prototype for suggestion—it is original in its
details.

GOUDY OPEN ITALIC
[Design No. 38]

THIS italic, intended of course to accompany Goudy
Open, is suitable also for use with Goudy Modern.
It found its first use in an article in *Ars Typographica*
in connection with Goudy Modern. It was an entirely new and original design that would go satisfactorily with many other types irrespective of the
roman it primarily was made to accompany. The
Monotype Company owns the reproduction rights;
the design itself is my property.

A B C D E F G H I J K L M N
O P Q R S T U V W X Y Y Z &
a b c d e f g h i j k l m n o p p q
r r s t u v w x y z . , ' ; : ! ? - G
fi ff ffi fl ffl $ 1 2 3 4 5 6 7 8 9 0

Speaking of earlier types,
Goudy says: The old fellows
stole all of our best ideas.

GOUDY ANTIQUE
[Design No. 39]

This design, begun in 1919, was first shown in drawings which were exhibited on the occasion of the A.I.G.A. printing show at the National Arts Club; I think this was in 1921. No patterns or matrices were cut until 1926, when I used some letters from it to form the word "Typographica" for the title-page of my type specimen No. 4, which presented the types I was prepared to furnish printers at that time.

This cutting represents my earliest attempts at matrix cutting at my newly-established foundry. In 1933, when Melbert Cary was preparing *The Story of the Village Type*, this face was used in the 12-point size (which, with the 14- and 18-point, I had cut in 1930), for the chronological list of my types which was printed therein. In an introduction to this list, I wrote: "In 1925, when I first began to think seriously of producing my own types, it was this type on which I began my experiments in making patterns . . . I tried out various materials and methods before finally evolving the master pattern I now use to produce a metal working pattern, from which the matrix itself is engraved."

My intention was to design a letter which would displace the monotonous "Antique Old Style" or "Bookman" faces. Of the same color or weight as these, the individual letters of my Antique show a greater variety in their forms.

On Thanksgiving Day, 1933, Bruce Rogers was at our home. He asked me what letter I might have that he could use on the title-page of his little *Champ Rosé*, which Peter Beilenson was printing for him; for the two title words, in the type he had planned to use, made too short a line in one size, and too long a line in the next size. We discussed my Antique (the name I had already given this face) but the same difficulty proved true of it in the existing sizes. He apparently dropped the matter; but while he was still chatting at the table, I went out to the shop, got out my Antique patterns, set the engraving machine and cut matrices for the letters required, in the exact size to give the length of line he wished—making the equivalent of about a 33-point face, which we could cast on a 36-point body. While I was engraving the matrices, my son Frederic had been heating up the caster, and the whole job, from discussion to cast type, was completed that afternoon. Some service!

Opposite the half-title on the three copies of *Champ Rosé* B.R. later gave me, appear these words: "We hereby give thanks to Frederic W. Goudy who on Thanksgiving Day cut the matrices and cast the principal type for the title of this book. B. R., P. B." —to which his name and Peter's are inscribed.

more by turning the leaves of the book of experience in their chosen trade than they would gain in the formal institutions established for that end. This is particularly true of the art of printing, as the elements of good expression and the thoughts of the best intellects are forced upon the minds of those who work at the composing-case. 1 2 3 4 5 6 7 8 9 0

ABCDEFGHIJKLMNOPQRSTVWXYZ&
abcdefghijklmnopqrstuvwxyzſtꜩﬁﬄﬂﬀﬃ.,':;?!

NABISCO
[Design No. 40]

In Chicago, in 1901 or 1902, I had hand-lettered the words "National Biscuit Company" for that concern. The commission came through their advertising executive, James Fraser, who did not tell me that twenty-five or more designers also had been given the same commission at the same time. A few days after I had delivered my drawing to Fraser, I received a telephone message from him requesting my presence at his office. On arriving there I was shown some forty other drawings of the same words I had drawn, and was then told that mine had won the competition. If I had known it was a competitive affair I might not have accepted the order at all, although *all* the drawings were to be paid for. One nice thing occurred when I presented my reasonable bill: Fraser surprised me by tearing it up in my presence, and asked me to make out another for double the amount.

Practically twenty years later, the New York advertising representatives of the company asked me to make a type for the National Biscuit Company, using letters of the character of those drawn so long before. I didn't like to tell them that I was not sure those letters were the sort that would make a *good* type to use for their announcements, booklets and advertisements; or that, since I had already made a type for the American Type Founders Company along the same lines, I feared any new attempt might prove too reminiscent of that type. However, I made drawings and had several sizes engraved by Wiebking. The Company named it "Nabisco" and used it frequently for booklets and small advertisements. Of late years I have not seen it so often, but I imagine it still is in occasional use.

In 1912 one day while seated at my desk on Madison Avenue, a man came in with a package under his arm. He said he was a lithographer, and had an order to reproduce a drawing which by constant use over a period of years was in pretty bad shape for satisfactory reproduction; he wondered if I could make a good copy of it for him. On opening the package I was amazed to find it was the original drawing I had made in Chicago in 1901 for the National Biscuit Company!

ABCDEFGHIJKLMNOP
QRSTUVWXYZabcdef
ghijklmnopqrstuvwxyz
$ & ?!'-.:;, 1 2 3 4 5 6 7 8 9 0

LINING GOTHIC
[Design No. 41]

THE drawings for this type were made with the thought of adding more interest to a design of this kind than is usually shown in the printers' "lining gothic"—or as we would probably say today, "sans-serif"—by varying some widths of characters and adding the merest suggestion of serifs to take away the hard and precise ending of the stems usually found in such type.

I sent the drawings to Wiebking, who for some reason did not cut the matrices as quickly as I thought he should, and so I recalled the drawings. Later I made patterns, intending to engrave the matrices myself; but due to the press of other work and probably loss of interest for that particular form of letter I did not get at them. I am egotistic enough to think that some of the commercial success of foreign sans-serif types like Kabel and Futura, which my design antedated, might have been mine if I had gone ahead with the cutting of the design.

One page of my *Elements of Lettering*, published in 1922, shows the letter as drawn; it is shown also in my revised and enlarged *Alphabet* issued by the University of California Press in 1942, and is here reproduced from that showing.

PACK MY BOX WITH

GARAMONT and ITALIC
[Designs No. 42 and No. 43]

In the fall of 1920, Mr. Dove, president of the Lanston Monotype Machine Company of Philadelphia, asked me if I would join that organization as their art advisor. After talking the matter over with Bertha, I decided to accept his suggestion although I had been "on my own" since 1900.

On one of my more or less regular visits to the factory to attend meetings to discuss new work, I suggested to Mr. Dove that there seemed to be a movement on the part of foundries to revive some of the old book types and "why should not the Monotype present its products first instead of following the others?" He asked for something more concrete and I said I would bring some sketches for a proposed new letter on my next visit.

I have the four-volume edition of Claudin's monumental *Histoire de l'Imprimerie en France au XV et XVI Siecle* in which the introduction is set in a large letter (about 24-point according to modern measurements) which was attributed to Claude Garamond (1540). I made drawings from this type and submitted them to Mr. Dove. I want here to set down authoritatively that most of the favorable criticism regarding my version of the type is misleading. Its final form as drawn by me was not the result of inspiration or of genius on my part, but was merely the result of an attempt to *reproduce* as nearly as possible the form and spirit of the "Garamond" letter. I made no attempt to eliminate the mannerisms or deficiencies of his famous type, realizing that they came not by intention, but rather through the punch-cutter's handling, to his lack of tools of precision and his crude materials; for he worked "by eye" and not by rule.

I did find it impossible to eliminate, in my own rendition of the letter, that subtle something we call "personality," that something made up of items so intangible as practically to be imperceptible when individual types are compared, yet clearly manifest when the page they form is viewed as a whole. The subtleties of "Garamond's" drawing I couldn't neglect, yet I did not *consciously* include them in my own drawings, and these are the touches that mark my face as belonging to the present and not to the sixteenth century.

A B C D E F G H I J K L M N O P
Q R S T U V W X Y Z & Æ Œ
A B C D E F G H I J K L M N O P Q R S T U
V W X Y Z & Æ Œ fi ff ffi fl ffl æ œ ct st
a b c d e f g h i j k l m n o p q r s t u v
w x y z . , ' ; : ! ? - [($ 1 2 3 4 5 6 7 8 9 0

Speaking of earlier types,
Goudy says: The old fellows
stole all of our best ideas.

Drawings like mine which were made free-hand, were not the sort usually worked from at the Monotype Company, so there was a constant fight to see that the workmen did not "correct" what seemed to them to be bad drawing on my part. If I intentionally gave a letter an inclination of one degree, they straightened it up. My serifs, which had a definite shape, were changed to meet their own ideas, since they "had always made them that way." Finally I went to Mr. Dove and complained that there was little point in my spending maybe hours to get a desired effect, only to have it nullified by a mere artisan's notion of what was right or wrong in my drawings. Mr. Dove thereupon gave orders that my drawings were to be followed *precisely*. One of the superintendents was heard to say that "if anyone bought that type, he must be a d——d fool." This same man, however, when hundreds of sets of mat-

A B C D E F G H I J K L M N O
P Q R S T U V W X Y Z & Æ Œ
a b c d e f g h i j k l m n o p q r s t u v w x y z
æ œ fi ff ffi fl ffl . , ' ; : ! ? - $ 1 2 3 4 5 6 7 8 9 0

Speaking of earlier types,
Goudy says: The old fellows
stole all of our best ideas.

rices of my face had been sold, later admitted to me that he was wrong.*

As all that I say herein regarding Garamont roman applies equally to the italic, I do not make a separate story about that face. For the italic I did make a few changes from the original types, where there seemed to me to be obvious slips in founding; changes in inclination, etc., rather than in design.

I suggested the name "Garamont" instead of "Garamond," as that name would show at once that it was a Monotype face, not to be confused with the faces of other concerns also following the same source. The name was found by me in *Notice sur les Types Etrangers du Specimen de l'Imprimerie Royale* about the type "attribuait à Garamont." "Garamont (Latin Garamontius) was used in books where he was named as the publisher." I have frequently been "corrected" by critics for my spelling of the word!

*A statement by the Monotype Company in *The Ben Franklin Monthly* for June, 1923, says that: "Within five weeks after mailing *Monotype*—the first commercial showing of this face—685 fonts had been sold."

GOUDY NEWSTYLE
[Design No. 44]

A LITTLE book came into my hands in 1920 which had been written by Robert Bridges, Poet Laureate of England, on a suggested revision of our ordinary roman alphabet, a revision which he thought would make it more easy for a foreigner to grasp the differences in words spelled differently but with the same pronunciation. Our English language abounds in such words; for example: *right*, the opposite of left; *rite*, a ceremony; *write*, to form letters or words as with a pen or pencil; and *wright*, a workman.

I was at that time preparing a series of essays on typography, legibility, the first types, and so on, and it occurred to me to add a chapter on "A new literary phonetic alphabet." I decided that to carry out Bridges' plan would prove more or less a makeshift, since he attempted to employ materials already in existence, but which were not always in complete harmony with the type alphabet into which he introduced them.

Bridges had laid down a premise that "it is usually held that any form of phonetic writing must be so dissimilar from the usual literary script as to be illegible without special study of its special symbols . . . on the other hand by choosing new symbols from among the various forms of the old alphabets, it is possible to construct a phonetic script which can be read by anyone acquainted with the ordinary English scripts."

As a designer of types I am not primarily concerned with the questions of phonetics; but with the question of legibility I am greatly concerned—that is, I am especially concerned with the production of a letter form that exactly and unequivocally expresses what letter it is, and I am only incidentally concerned with its sound or the sounds it represents. My intention, therefore, was to attempt to carry out something of Bridges' idea in a more practical form to make pronunciation generally more easy, but not at the expense of easy readability.

I soon found that any plan which would go far enough to be of real value would also be too radical for ready acceptance by readers; I therefore decided to attempt something more simple, but still something that would have value and which would not require too much special study to grasp.

The written (printed) word constitutes the continuity of language and of learning and provides for its permanence. A literary phonetic alphabet does

A B C D E F G H I J K L M N
O P Q R S T U V W X Y Z &
a b c d e f g h i j k l m n o p q r s t
u v w x y z ff fl ffl & . , ' ; : ! ? -
1 2 3 4 5 6 7 8 9 0

Speaking of earlier types, Goudy says:
The old fellows stole all of our best ideas.

not necessarily imply or require phonetic spelling. In English it sometimes happens that two words have the same pronunciation as well as the same spelling; in these "homonyms" we have the same letters but entirely different meanings; thus, "league," a treaty, from *ligare*, to bind; "league" from *leuca*, a measure of distance; here a phonetic alphabet would serve no purpose.

Then there is a different class of words which are pronounced the same but spelled differently; these "homophones" spelled phonetically would break the visible connection between them and the words from which they are descended, thus bite, bight; pique, peak, peek; reign, rein, rain; in such cases little would be gained by a phonetic alphabet. But for those words spelled alike but *pronounced* differently, a new alphabet would fix instantly the different pronunciation, and for those words with identical combinations of letters but which vary in pronunciation, a phonetic alphabet would prove useful; thus (ange)r, (ange)l; h(eight), (eight); (choi)r, (choi)ce, etc.

The alphabet consists of twenty-six letters represented by two forms, capitals and minuscules (lower-case), and of these two forms some differ so greatly that it is necessary to learn them individually —only eight being so similar in form that to learn one is to know the other; C c, I i, J j, Kk, Oo, P p, S s, Zz. In all, forty forms are required to represent twenty-six letters.

It occurred to me that it would be very worth while to design an alphabet that could be read by anyone, but which at the same time would make pronunciation more easy. It could be done in part by adding a few extra letters to indicate the hard or soft sounds of g, the long or short sounds of a, e, i, etc. Take, for example, the words "anger" and "danger": what is there to differentiate the two pronunciations of g? But if we print

anger   danger

the different pronunciations are clearly indicated.*

I thereupon drew an alphabet to which I added twenty-odd alternate forms, and had Wiebking cut the type for me in 18-point, but I never got around to making any general use of the added quaint characters. The face itself I named "Goudy Newstyle." Its first important showing was in a book for the Grolier Club. The Grabhorns have used it successfully in a number of books, notably the monumental *Leaves of Grass*, Washington's *Farewell Address*, and the handsome folio *A Brief History of Japanese Color Prints*. As I had cut it in only one size, it did not sell largely. When some of the matrices were accidentally damaged, I decided to make new patterns, and I personally recut the face in 1935 (without the special characters) in the 12-, 14-, and 18-point sizes. In the Typophile volume *Barnacles from Many Bottoms* I used the 14-point size for "Retrospectus," an open letter to Bruce Rogers, in which I said: "This letter is set in one of my types which I think you like. I have made new patterns and cut matrices especially for this tribute; the face, in a

*These additional characters were to be of forms already familiar to readers, but made to harmonize in weight and line with the types into which they would be introduced.

sense, by its use here, is dedicated to you in honor of your outstanding achievements in typography."

In 1942 I sold the design to the Monotype Company, who will bring it out after the war is won.

"If (as Morris once said) I were not so damned old," I would again attempt a new "literary pho-. netic" alphabet.

PHILOBIBLON A RICARDO
pars capituli ⋅ de commendatione ientia habitat.

AM veritas vocis perit cum so absconsa et thesaurus invisus: ve se disciplinali sensui manifestare dum aucitur, amplius vero et tadt

GOUDY ITALIC
[Design No. 45]

After coming into repossession of the drawings
made for Louis H. Orr of the Bartlett-Orr Press, I
decided that an italic would be necessary if and when
the Orr type ever was cut, and drawings were made.
Unfortunately no patterns were made and of the face
nothing remains except the note regarding it in *The
Story of the Village Type* chronology: "Exists as
drawings. To accompany No. 23."

ITALIAN OLD STYLE and ITALIC
[Designs No. 46 and No. 47]

ON ONE of my regular trips to the Monotype Company in Philadelphia, the then president, Mr. Dove, told me that the Company had a tentative order for two complete monotype equipments, provided they could supply matrices for Cloister Old Style as a part of the type equipment. My reply was, in substance, that the Cloister face was owned by the American Type Founders Company, who had developed it by expensive advertising until it was in great demand, and I didn't think the Monotype ought deliberately to purloin a rival concern's property.

Although Mr. Dove said he felt that all foundries' types were largely obtained by copying or adapting the types of other concerns here, or from foreign sources, and that therefore the Monotype would only be following customary practices if they put Cloister on their machine, he asked me to suggest an alternative type that would make the sale. I said that Cloister was based on, or practically copied from, the type designed in Venice by Nicolas Jenson about 1470; so why not go back to the types of that time and, using one of them as a basis, make a face of the same general character as Jenson's, which would serve today's uses as well as Cloister, but which would not be in any sense a copy or an imitation of it?

Mr. Dove admitted that he was not posted on early types and wanted something more concrete. I told him that on my next trip to Philadelphia I would bring with me enlarged drawings of Jenson's letter, and also some drawings of the types of Jenson's contemporaries. I would also make some sketches of a letter such as I had in mind which would serve the same purpose as Cloister, but at the same time give the Monotype a standing as an originator rather than as an imitator of any other concern's productions. I carried out my promise as to Jenson, etc., and also made careful drawings of the suggested new face, and was pleased to have Mr. Dove tell me to go ahead with my idea.

Italian Old Style, which I called my new letter, is not an adaptation or copy of any of the early Italian faces, though of course it shows study of them. The individual letters are quite full and round and with their close fitting give an impression of luxuriousness combined with legibility, simplicity and dignity.

Bruce Rogers, who was engaged to make the dis-

A B C D E F G H I J K L M
N O P Q R S T U V W X Y
Z & . , ' ; : ! ? - fi ff ffi fl ffl ﬀ ﬆ ℭ
a b c d e f g h i j k l m n o p q r s
t u v w x y z $ 1 2 3 4 5 6 7 8 9 0

Speaking of earlier types,
Goudy says: The old fellows
stole all of our best ideas.

tinguished specimen showing of the roman and italic, said of it that it "reminds me strongly and admirably of Ratdolt's fine roman."* Mr. Rogers used as copy for the specimen showing a conversation from Dibdin's *Bibliographical Decameron* and produced a publicity pamphlet worthy of a more ambitious subject. I have as his gift the dummy of the booklet showing his meticulous care for endless details. William Edwin Rudge printed the specimen in masterly fashion. One advertising company had written of Italian Old Style that "they were sorry it wasn't adapted to their work," but the Rogers booklet changed their minds and they later made large use of it.

It is interesting to note that while copies of the booklet could be obtained without charge from the

*A B C C D E E F G H I J K L L M
N O P Q Q R S T T U V U W X
Y Z & . , ' ; : ! ? - fi ff ffi fl ffl Et st
a b c d e f g h i j k l m n o p q r s
t u v w x y z $ 1 2 3 4 5 6 7 8 9 0*

*Speaking of earlier types,
Goudy says: The old fellows
stole all of our best ideas.*

*It was not, however, based on Ratdolt's letter.

Monotype Company, copies of it were also being sold by certain book dealers, located only a few blocks away, as examples of Rogersiana!

I was pleased when B.R. chose Italian Old Style to set the descriptive matter in the title-page border of his fine Grolier Club edition of Tory's *Champ Fleury*. The text was set in Rogers' Centaur type, and my recollection is that at the time of its publication (1927) he had only the 14-point size available —but this was too large to get in all of the matter included in the Tory title page, and he found my type would go in the space and harmonize with his text type.

KENNERLEY BOLD and
KENNERLEY BOLD ITALIC
[Designs No. 48 and No. 49]

OF these types there isn't much to record. It has long been the fashion among founders to take a book face and add weight enough to it to make a bold face to give emphasis to words or lines in connection with the normal weight. There would be no difficulty in doing this, if the weight could be added in direct proportion to the *height and width* of each letter; but to be used together in the same line with normal type, the *height* of the normal must be preserved, leaving only the width to carry the weight. Thus the new letter is thrown out of proportion, and preserves little more than a suggestion of the regular face. A bold type should be drawn "bold" at the outset without reference to any other type, if proportion is to be preserved.

ABCDEFGHIJKLMNOPQ
RSTUVWXYZ& fi ff ffi fl ffl
abcdefghijklmnopqrstuvw
xyzctst.,';:!?-($1234567890

Speaking of earlier types,
Goudy says: The old fellows
stole all of our best ideas.

Kennerley Bold and Italic were drawn for use with Kennerley Old Style in words or lines requiring special emphasis, or by themselves when color in the mass is required. As the individual characters are not unduly expanded, in spite of the added weight, they make a solid readable page, or display lines not too black when used with more delicate faces. Kennerley Bold and Bold Italic have virility without crudity, and are adapted to simple, compact composition with a quality of bold readability. The New York Telephone Company uses it frequently in its newspaper advertising.

I think I kept the Kennerley character in my bold rendition as well as could be done, but I fear it never had the vogue Monotype hoped for it.

A B C D E F G H I J K L M N
O P Q R S T U V W X Y Z &
a b c d e f g h i j k l m n o p q r s t u
v w x y z . , ' ; : ! ? - $ 1 2 3 4 5 6 7 8 9 0

Speaking of earlier types,
Goudy says: The old fellows
stole all of our best ideas.

GOUDY HEAVY FACE and ITALIC
[Designs No. 50 and No. 51]

AFTER Mr. Dove's death, Harvey Best became president of the Lanston Monotype Machine Company. While he had been Mr. Dove's assistant I had come in close contact with him and we frequently discussed, in a free and informal manner, items for future Monotype production. He was quite obsessed with the idea that a very heavy black type would be a good seller and he brought up the question of such a design quite often. As such a letter has little appeal to me I was slow in getting at it, but finally I did. I am quite certain that my design was more or less a disappointment to Best, although he put through an

ABCDEFGHIJKLMN
OPQRSTUVWXYZ&
abcdefghijklmnopqrs
tuvwxyzfifffffiflfflctst
.,';:!?-$1234567890

Speaking of earlier types, Goudy says: The old fellows stole all of our best ideas.

order for cutting it. He would, I know, have liked a letter blacker even than the one I made, although I endeavored to show him that to make stems, etc., much heavier than I had, would leave practically no white at all in the "counters"—the open areas inside such letters as a, b, d, e, A, B, D, O, etc.

Of the Heavy Face I said: "it is an original face designed to meet a growing demand for emphatic types for display . . . It has greater weight or color than can be obtained with most of the bold faces, but without freaky or flamboyant features." All I say here regarding the roman applies equally to the italic I made to accompany it.

ABCÇDEFGHIJKL
MMNOPPQRSTU
VUWXYZ&.,';:!?-
abcdefgghijklmno
pqrstuvwxyzfiffffi
flffl$1234567890

**Speaking of earlier
types, Goudy says:
The old fellows stole
all of our best ideas.**

MARLBOROUGH
[Design No. 52]

THIS letter was made on the assumption that it was
to be used for a specific book, but when the matrices
were finished I found that the printer who was doing
the printing, and who also was to publish the book,
had gone ahead with the composition using an existing type without waiting for the one I was making for it. This left me with a type on my hands
which I did not especially need at this time.

Wiebking had cut it for me in 16-point. My
drawings were made on a nine-inch basis and I did
not realize at that time that some features of such
large letters, when reduced to type size, would more
or less disappear. Just why I made nine-inch drawings for this face I am not quite certain, unless it
was that I already had decided to use this dimension
in preparing my own patterns for the matrix engraving I was planning soon to take up. Later I did use
this size for my master patterns, until I found that a
7½ inch size would give me just as good results and
would be easier to make.

I cast up some fonts of Marlborough but did not
push the sales, as I planned some revisions in those

A B C D E F G H I J K L M N O P
Q R S T U V W X Y Z & . , ' ; : ! ? -
a b c d e f g h i j k l m n o p q r s t u v w x
y z æ œ fi ff ffi fl ffl ꝯt $ 1 2 3 4 5 6 7 8 9 0

features which did not satisfy me: one feature especially, the serifs, came out entirely too weak in the type. I had made most of my intended revisions on the drawings, but never got around to making new patterns before the 1939 fire; consequently nothing remains to show what changes I contemplated, although they are quite clear in my own mind.

In 1942 I sold the design (as shown by proofs of it), to the Monotype Company, with the understanding that I would either make or suggest the intended changes when the Company would be able to start work on it—work until now prevented by war conditions. The type was given the name "Marlborough" after the name of the town where it was designed. I do not think the town itself was ever aware of the "honor" paid it!

VENEZIA ITALIC
[Design No. 53]

IN the spring of 1925, the late George W. Jones, England's well-known printer, and typographic counsellor to the English Linotype Company, wrote me asking the cost of an italic to accompany his "Venezia" face; and after some correspondence I received an order to go ahead with the drawings.

Nicolas Jenson, celebrated for the Roman type, was according to legend, sent to Mainz by Charles VII of France, who thought that his Tours mint-master should acquaint himself with a sufficient amount of knowledge of the new printing art, to use it to advantage upon his return. (1458)

De Præparatione Evangelica of Eusebius is generally considered Jenson's first book.

A B C D E F G H I J K L M N O P
Q R S T U V W X Y Z Æ Œ

a b c d e f g h i j k l m n o p q r s
t u v w x y z æ œ

1 2 3 4 5 6 7 8 9 0 £ , : ; ' ' (-) ! ? &

I was in England later in the year, and took over with me the drawings I had made. They evidently pleased Jones because he sent me a draft for the reasonable bill I rendered; but he did not commission me to engrave matrices for the face, although he had asked the cost of that work also. I later discovered that the English Linotype Company had produced the Italic. I am under the impression that Mr. Jones transferred both the roman and italic Venezia to the Linotype Company. The type shown is a reproduction from a proof Jones sent to me.

Stanley Morison (in error) says of it that "this italic is based upon an early French renaissance fount, that *cut by Claude Garamond circa 1535.*" *If* it has any resemblance whatever to Garamond's letter, it is purely coincidental, as I insist I made it to accompany the roman *without reference to any other letter* except the roman it was to complement..

ARIES
[Design No. 54]

SHORTLY after beginning work at my newly-established Village Letter Foundry in 1925, Spencer Kellogg, of Eden, New York, began operating his new private press, and for it he placed large orders for types I was casting and offering to printers—in fact, his orders embarrassed me by their size, as I was not as yet equipped for large output.

On one of Kellogg's visits to Marlboro, he suggested that he might like a private type for his "Aries Press." My first thought was to make for him a letter based upon the classic forms of the early Venetians, and sketches were begun along this line and *approved* by him, but on the occasion of a later visit to my workshop, a suggestion was made— whether by me or by him, I do not remember—that a type with some qualities not generally found in the early Italian types might be a pleasing variation, since the type he wanted was intended for printing texts in limited editions, texts that in themselves would not be ordinary.

We talked over the types of the private presses and finally decided that a face with the color and mass effect of the Subiaco used by St. John Hornby at his famous Ashendene Press was the sort that offered possibilities for a new letter. The first sketches I had made for a roman thereupon were scrapped and drawings for a new "old face" were begun. This was in the summer of 1925.

I had purchased an engraving machine; I could not purchase also the mechanical knack needed to use it, a knack which comes only from experience; so it was a really chancy undertaking for me to attempt (with no previous matrix cutting experience) the engraving of a hundred or more matrices. Records of progress at this time were not kept consistently, but by noting dates that occasionally appeared on drawings or proofs, I find that my first pencil drafts are dated November 8, 1925, and by November 22 my drawings in ink were completed. And then began the travail of accomplishment.

Drawings were easy to make, but how to translate drawings into patterns from which to cut matrices? Some sort of pattern was essential, and a record of those I attempted shows that more than one hundred and fifty were made; at first some letters were cut laboriously from hard fibre sheets about one-sixteenth of an inch thick, which were then mounted with Lepage's glue on other sheets of the same fibre, making enlarged sunken patterns for use in producing reduced metal working patterns; for others, letters were cut from heavy Bristol board and likewise mounted, but this material proved not too satisfactory. I finally found that a hard drawing paper, three or four ply, gave me the best results, and I have used it for all of my master-pattern work since.

Then came the matter of grinding engraving tools that would cut a sunken matrix in hard brass or German silver fifty-odd thousandths of an inch deep; the preparation of the matrix blanks; the thousand and one things necessary before a single matrix could be cut; and the repeated experiments, all of which required considerable time—so that it was well into 1926 before I was able to show proofs of some seventy characters.

As might be expected, these first proofs showed inequalities in weight, line, etc., yet on the whole I believe they were probably as successful as the first efforts of many of the early craftsmen starting from "scratch." Corrections, recuttings, changes, took time, and my customer, tiring of his press in the meantime, shut up shop—throwing the type back on my hands. What finally became of the 500-odd pounds of 16-point type I had shipped to him, I do not know.

The information contained in this account of the Aries face has been taken from notes prepared prior to the fire in 1939. I have written at length because the work on this face represents the principal beginnings of my typefounding experience, and until now has never been put into print.

Details of the later development and ownership of the face appear in the account herein of another type, No. 81.

I SCOWRETH all scurfe and scalds from the head, being therewith dailie washt before meales. Being moderatlie taken [saith he] it sloweth age, it strengtheth youth, it helpeth digestion, it cutteth flegme, it lighteneth the mind, it quickeneth the spirits, it cureth the hydropsie, it healeth the Strangurie, it pounceth the stone, it expelleth gravel, it puffeth aways all ventositie, it keepeth and preserveth the head from whirling, the eies from dazeling, the toong from lisping, the mouth from maffling, the teeth from chattering, and the throte from ratling; it keepeth the weasan from stifling, the stomach from wambling, and the heart from swelling, the bellie from wirtching, the guts from numbling, the hands from shivering, & the sinews from

GOUDY DUTCH
[Design No. 55]

THE origin of this face was some handwriting on an envelope addressed to me by a correspondent in Holland. The script was so unusual in character that I immediately conceived the notion of making a type with it as a foundation. I practically completed the drawings; to carry out successfully all of the possibilities that suggested themselves required a considerable technical skill that at the moment seemed beyond me, such as the cutting of several matrices of different point sizes to be cast and combined in one line to produce the effect I wished and the design never got beyond the drawing stage. I have regretted the loss of these drawings keenly, although they might have proved too radical to have made a popular type.

COMPANION OLD STYLE
and ITALIC
[Designs No. 56 and No. 57]

Henry B. Quinan, then art director for the *Woman's Home Companion*, asked me to quote him a price for furnishing the Crowell Publishing Company a type for use for the headings of the *Companion*, in roman and italic. Up to this time I had not succeeded in making a matrix expeditiously nor satisfactorily in every detail, although I had succeeded finally in cutting over a hundred mats for the Aries face previously described.

My first drawings for the new Crowell letter, which I had shown to Quinan on one of his visits to my shop, did not seem to me to "fill the bill" entirely as to the sort of letter a woman's magazine would find sufficiently distinctive, and while Quinan did not definitely disapprove of the design, I sensed a certain disappointment or dissatisfaction on his

A B C D E F G H I J K L M N O P
Q R S T U V W X Y Z & . , '; : ! ? -

ABCDEFGHIJKLMNOPQRSTUVWXYZ
a b c d e f g h i j k l m n o p q r s t u v
w x y z fi ff ffi fl ffl 1 2 3 4 5 6 7 8 9 0

Speaking of earlier types, Goudy says:
The old fellows stole all of our best i

part. I thereupon scrapped my drawings and *without* further consultation with him started new drawings from a different viewpoint, making patterns and engraving a specimen in 24-point, proofs of which I offered for his approval. I believe the new letter I showed him, both in the roman and italic, is one of the most distinctive types I have ever made. It incorporates features which deliberately violate tradition as to stress of curves, but which are so handled that attention is not specifically drawn to the innovations introduced. It was a strong letter, yet not too bold for a magazine intended for women's reading.

The order was placed with me in 1927, but my first proof was dated March 11, 1928. The Crowell Company was patient and did not press me unduly (they did not know that I was learning the business of type-founding while working on its face). There is practically no place outside a type foundry where one can learn the "mystery" of matrix engraving, nor any books treating of the subject which

ABCDEFGHIJKLMNOPQRS TUVWXYZ&abcdefghijklm nopqrstuvwxyz fi ff ffi fl ffl .,';:!?- A B C D E M P R g ct z

Speaking of earlier types, Goudy says: The old fellows stole all of our best ideas.

really help the beginner, so I had to start from scratch.

To make cutting tools meant experimenting hour after hour, discarding tool after tool, noting in each what seemed unsatisfactory, changing angles of the cutting edges, etc., until one joyous day I found I had succeeded in grinding a cutter which not only would cut clean, but with which I could control the width of the line being cut. This meant that I had finally succeeded in making a cutting tool that would, if necessary, cut a line one-and-one-half thousandths of an inch in width and still be strong enough to cut a depth of fifty-odd thousandths of an inch in hard brass or German silver without breaking.

I say "one joyous day"—it was joyous enough as to accomplishment, but tempered somewhat by the fact that I discovered I had lost the sight of my right eye overnight and I must perforce go on thereafter handicapped by imperfect sight in the performance of a craft in which even perfect sight is not quite good enough!

The new 24-point proofs pleased Mr. Quinan and the magazine editors, and I went about the work of engraving matrices for their design—I think I cut all the sizes from 10-point to 42-point, roman and italic. From types cast in my matrices, the Monotype Company made electro matrices for the printers of the magazine.

The face was used in the magazine for some years until the demand for more bizarre forms became general. I believe that Companion Old Style and its italics show greater consistent *original* features than any other face I have ever made.

DEEPDENE
[Design No. 58]

THIS year (1927) was a prolific one for me. I find that I was working on six different designs. For one of them I began drawings of a type suggested by a Dutch type which had just been introduced into this country; but as with some of my previous designs, I soon got away from my exemplar to follow a line of my own. I showed my drawings to the Monotype Company—but they said they were not then interested in a new book face.

By September, 1927, I had engraved the matrices for the 24-point capitals, and the 18-, 16-, and 14-point capitals and lower-case; and with the help of Peter Beilenson (the printer of the present volume, who was working with me at this time), produced a broadside on the hand press showing these sizes, which the Continental Typefounders Association offered for sale. It announced that the 12-, 30-, 36-,

A B C D E F G H I J K L M N O P
Q R S T U V W X Y Z & . , ' ; : ! ? -

ABCDEFGHIJKLMNOPQRSTUVWXYZ&

a b c d e f g h i j k l m n o p q r s t u v
w x y z fi ff ffi fl ffl [ ] 1 2 3 4 5 6 7 8 9 0

Speaking of earlier types, Goudy says:
The old fellows stole all of our best ideas.

150

and lower-case for the 24-point sizes were in preparation, also that an italic in all sizes was planned. Beilenson also set in the 16-point size, and printed in my shop, *Two Singers*, a book of poems by Charles Hanson Towne, to be published by William Edwin Rudge; for the title I designed and engraved the types for the word "Singers" shown here.

SINGERS

One day shortly after my showing of the face Rudge telephoned me asking me to have luncheon with him at the Transportation Club, in New York City. He said he liked "Deepdene" (the name I had given the design—naming it after my modest estate at Marlboro), and would like to get it for his own use if I would consider parting with it. He said he would want, of course, an italic to accompany it. We talked the matter over and I set a price which was satisfactory to him. He said he would give me a definite answer in the course of a week or so; in about two weeks we met again at the same club and he said he was ready to go ahead with the transaction, but he would want also a bold face to go with it, and how much more would that add to the price agreed on? As he wanted drawings only for the bold I named a nominal sum. He then said he would want the Mergenthaler Linotype Company to make matrices for him.

I told him that I could not consider the Linotype

at all in the deal, as I was under contract with the Monotype Company and could not draw for any composing machine other than the Monotype; but if he would get Mr. Best's consent I would let him have the design. This Best would not agree to; he was, in fact, quite angry with me, as he had the impression I was willing to dicker with the Linotype Company contrary to the business arrangement between the Monotype and me.

When I explained that I had only agreed to sell to Rudge *personally* (and I did not then know that he was a typographic consultant of the Linotype), Best asked if I would give Monotype the reproduction rights—for which he would make me a liberal advance on royalties. This arrangement suited me and the first sales of matrices were very satisfactory.

I have always resented the fact that when Deepdene was put on the Monotype machine I was not asked to cooperate in adapting the individual characters to the die-case, for I feel that the slight changes made do not always carry out my own ideas as to the changes necessary, or as to the fitting of those changed characters.

When Simon & Shuster issued their edition of *The Bible as Living Literature* they used Deepdene and its italics, but the publisher's note about the design of the type seems to me to suggest that my design was somehow at fault. It states that the book "is set in 14-point Deepdene, a contemporary book face designed by Frederic W. Goudy for the Lanston Monotype Machine Company, Philadelphia, Pennsylvania. Many of the characters have been recut and refitted for the special purposes of this text."

In the first place Deepdene was *not* designed for the Monotype, as I have said; I made it for my own use and for sale to printers, and for this purpose I cut the first matrices. I presume the note in the S. & S. Bible specifically means that the changes were made to adapt the face to the die-case, but it reads as though the Monotype or the publishers felt it necessary or desirable to improve my design. At any rate I am glad the use of it did not prevent the publishers from selling several hundred thousand copies of the Good Book!

RECORD TITLE
[Design No. 59]

EARLY in 1927 I was talking to the late Hal March-banks at his Press on East 13th Street. A gentleman came in to whom Hal introduced me. His name was Charles DeVinne; and he was the grandson (I think) of Theodore L. DeVinne.

DeVinne was art director of *The Architectural Record*. He asked whether the *Record* might get a type of its own for its headings; and if so, how much would such a type cost; and also how long a time would I require—could the type be finished before the end of the year? I made a quick quotation for design, cutting matrices in four sizes, and a price per pound for the type I would supply and assured him that the work could be done in time.

I suggested that for an architectural publication something based on the monumental lapidary inscriptions of the early Romans would be appropriate; and such a letter would harmonize with almost any good type used for the text of the magazine. His reply was that the character of the type "was up to me" as I was supposed to know about such matters. In a few days a letter came telling me to go ahead with the work.

Some time before this conversation I had purchased a reprint by Stanley Morison of a newly-discovered treatise on classic letter design originally printed at Parma by Damianus Moyllus about 1480, a treatise which gave the geometrical proportions of an alphabet of roman capitals. I wondered whether capitals like those shown therein would be a good basis for a heading type for the *Record*, and I began drawings along these lines.

I soon found that when they were reduced to type many modifications were imperative, and in some letters decided changes in form were necessary to fit them for use to modern eyes.

Certain features had to be exaggerated or they would disappear in the cutting; curves needed strengthening, stems and hair lines needed to be thickened or brought into greater harmony with each other. In addition, these letters of Moyllus were mathematically constructed, with every vertical line exactly the same width as every horizontal line, and such letter construction takes little account of those optical illusions on which, the experienced designer knows, depend the fine and almost imperceptible qualities which mean so much to the appearance of the type *in the mass*. An architect knows that a vertical line does not give the same impression of width as a horizontal line actually of the same width.

DeVinne did not press me, but within a couple of months (early in July, in fact) I was able to show him a proof of the 24-point size complete. I had not shown him any drawings, so this proof was his first sight of my design. Evidently it was entirely satisfactory, as the only word I got from the magazine was a check for one-half the total amount I was to receive, with a request to finish other sizes as soon as practicable. A proof (fortunately saved from the fire) showing practically all the 12-, 14-, and 18-point characters, is, I note, dated December 18, 1927.

This was one of the most satisfactory commissions I ever undertook. For the May 1928 issue of the magazine I laid out the cover design, using the new type, and "blowing it up" for the two large lines of the title; and I contributed also, by request, an article on the design of types which described the magazine's new letter, with illustrations from Moyllus, my *Alphabet*, and a reproduction of one of my working drawings.

The magazine used my type for several years until the craze for sans serifs came in and widely displaced the ordinary roman forms.

IMP·CAESARI DIVI
NERVAE TRAIANO OPTI
ICO DACICO PONT MAX
IMP VII COS VI PP FORTISSIMO

GOUDY UNCIALS
[Design No. 60]

For these letters I planned to take capitals, based more or less on the mediaeval scribes' capitals, and to enclose each in a square, making the letter white on a solid background. These were to be used as initial letters. I finished the drawings, made a few patterns, but never got around to cutting any matrices. The chronological list in *The Story of The Village Type* mentions them, and that "mention" is all that remains regarding design or patterns, which were completely lost in the 1939 fire.

DEEPDENE ITALIC
[Design No. 61]

DEEPDENE roman was made in 1927, and when the Monotype took over the reproduction rights for it, an italic was called for.

The italic I made, in its lower-case at least, owes little to historic forms (excepting only to the Aldine character to which, in my opinion, all true italics hark). Although made to accompany Deepdene roman, I hoped it would be found worthy to stand alone, just as the older italics were intended to stand. I chose more or less to disregard tradition in an attempt to follow a line of my own, and drew each character without reference to any other craftsman's work. I think this italic shows a disciplined freedom which retains the essential quality of legibility.

The capitals present no radical departures from traditional forms—indeed they could not without danger of eccentricity, but the swash characters I added give the capitals a degree of variety and a

ABCDEFGHIJKLMNOPQRS
TUVWXYZ& abcdefghijklm
nopqrstuvwxyzfiffffiflffl& .,';:!?-
ABCDEGMPRJ kzg gg gg gy

Speaking of earlier types, Goudy says:
The old fellows stole all of our best ideas.

157

touch of elegance which relieves the face from any tendency toward undue primness.

Notwithstanding the slight inclination of the letters it is a true italic, since after all an italic is not so much a matter of inclination as of innate character.

For the 24-point used in the first specimen of Deepdene Italic, Mrs. Goudy, who had learned the use of the matrix engraving machine, cut the matrices and did them as well as I could have done.*

On page 100 of Bruce Rogers' book *Paragraphs on Printing*, he says of italic figures that "Some printing-offices even make it a part of their shop style not to use italic figures under any circumstances; yet this is unsound because some of the most interesting and graceful numerals can be found in italic founts." I am reminded on reading his statement that for his little book *Letters From T. E. Shaw*, which Bertha set for him in 16-point Deepdene Italic, I had at his request designed and engraved matrices for italic figures for use with the italic text. I also cast, for use in this book, Deepdene Italic capitals in 14-point to line with the 16-point lowercase, and cut also a simpler form of cap T and, I think, an N. These special characters have never appeared elsewhere. And speaking of these types for B.R., I recall revising slightly some Deepdene Italic swash characters drawn by Richard Ellis for the book *Translations from the Chinese*, by Arthur Waley, which were cut for him by the Monotype.

---

*I used this 24-point to present my "Evening at Deepdene," beautifully printed by Howard Coggeshall at his Press in Utica.

GOUDY TEXT
[Design No. 62]

Aᴛᴇʀ my little foundry had gotten well under way, it occurred to me that I had no black-letter type among my stock of designs. Some years earlier I had purchased a leaf of the Gutenberg 42-line Bible, the first important book printed from movable types. This page is set in a strong, virile type, an imitation of the then current Teutonic manuscript hands; the page abounds in contractions, abbreviations, and ligatures to conserve space and approximate the vagaries and whimsicalities of the scribes' handling. For my new type I wanted a gothic letter that would give me the solid effect of that famous Gutenberg letter but if possible without its mannerisms.

Some time before 1920 I had made a cover design for the Marchbanks Press for a pamphlet to be printed at the Press to advertise Dill & Collins' new paper "Canterbury Book." For the title I had lettered the words "Canterbury Book" in a black letter, using Lombardic forms of "C" and "B" as initials. In May 1922 my book *Elements of Lettering* was published by Mitchell Kennerley. In it I showed drawings for a black-letter based on the lettering of the Dill & Collins pamphlet cover.

In 1927, for my title line of *Typographica No. 5*, I cut out individual letters from a proof of an *Elements* reproduction and pasted them up to form the word. When I began my drawings for the projected new type these examples came to mind and I decided that the letters shown in my *Elements of Lettering* might practically be copied. They were the result of study of early Gothic forms of the scribes, and of the types of Ratdolt and his contemporaries.

Of the design as finally cut, I wrote that "it is a freely rendered Gothic letter, composite in form from various sources. This sort of letter being less perfect in form than the roman character, lends itself to a greater variety in design." Its first appearance was in a Christmas card which I set in the 18-point size. This card attracted the attention of Mr. Best, president of Monotype, and he asked permission to put it on the machine. He wished to change my name "Goudy Black" to "Goudy Text," the name by which it is now known. For a showing of it the Company prepared an elaborate eight-page pamphlet in three colors, showing sizes 10- to 72-point. Unfortunately for my own peace of mind, the cover for this pamphlet exploits my name in 72-point with a *cipher* in "Goudy" instead of the letter "o." I regret also that the fitting of some of the characters was somewhat carelessly done in its production of the face.

I myself made a *faux pas*—my drawings show a "trait" on the lower-case b, h, k, l, which properly belongs only to the "l." The "trait" is a little pointed projection on the left of the straight stem of the "l" at the height of the lower-case "middles" and (I think) was used to differentiate the "l" from the figure one (1). In my ignorance I put a trait on the other straight ascending stems where it was not needed, a lapse I never expect to live down, although no one, as yet, has called me for it—praise be!

The late Melbert B. Cary, Jr., once told me that he had a letter from a well-known German printer

160

who intimated that "he could see how a German might have designed Goudy Text, but he couldn't see how an American could do it." There must be some "Goth" in my blood.

𝕬𝕭𝕮𝕯𝕰𝕱𝕲𝕳𝕴𝕵𝕶𝕷𝕸𝕹
𝕺𝕻𝕼𝕽𝕾𝕿𝖀𝖁𝖂𝖃𝖄𝖅
abcdefghijklmnopqrstuvwxyz
& $ffl fl fi ff ffi . : ; - , ' ?! 1234567890

Speaking of earlier types, Goudy says: The old fellows stole all of our

STRATHMORE TITLE
[Design No. 63]

STRATHMORE TITLE really doesn't belong in this list of types, as it was made for my own convenience in preparing a booklet for the Strathmore Paper Company's "Old Stratford" paper. The entire alphabet was drawn, but for the title of the booklet I made patterns and cut matrices only for the letters A, B, D, E, F, H, K, L, M, O, P, R, S, T, intending to complete the set of matrices at some later date.

STRATHMORE
OLD STRATFORD
BOOK PAPERS

LOMBARDIC CAPITALS
[Design No. 64]

The Story of the Village Type chronology shows the date for the drawings of these Lombardic letters as 1921, and that for the cutting of the matrices as 1929. I imagine the earlier date refers to the showing made in *Elements of Lettering* before the thought of cutting the design in type occurred to me. I find by comparison that my type forms differ slightly here and there from the *Elements* version, but do follow those earlier drawings in the main.

The Lombardic letters were a development by the Italians of the old roman cursive letters. Most of the types based on them are too stiff and formal to grace the page where used; in drawing mine I kept this fact in mind and attempted also to make forms less ornate than some of the original painted letters, which frequently lost their typical characteristics, and showed a tendency to confusion and illegibility, by being fattened vulgarly and overburdened with ornament. Lombardic Capitals may properly serve as alternate letters to replace the usual black-letter capitals when a touch of elegance is desirable. Used by themselves they do not usually combine well in words or sentences, and they were not intended to be so used.

ABCDEFGHIJKL
MNOPQRSTUVW
XYZ

SANS SERIF HEAVY
[Design No. 65]

THIS type was made for the Monotype Company and, to me, proved somewhat disappointing when produced; I fear it was a disappointment also to the Company, as I do not see it frequently in print. The most I can say for it is that it is a simple, sincere effort to provide a sans-serif letter that might hold its own in the revival of sans-serifs brought in from English and German foundries some years ago.

As a matter of fact sans-serifs have a very respectable lineage, reaching for their beginnings even further into the dim past than the roman letters, which, although they spring from the same sources, have developed along different lines.

Foundries usually listed these letters as "lining gothics" and usually showed capital forms only; occasionally a lower-case was added, not always in complete harmony with the capitals.

Without reference, however, to the classic Greek models of these lining gothics, I attempted to give to my type a definite expression of freedom and a personal quality not always found in this kind of letter. My type, in the nature of things, could offer few radical differences in forms when compared with dozens of similar types, but I did hope to incorporate subtle variations in proportions and handling of details not found in those previously listed in the specimen books. Evidently I didn't succeed too well.

KAATSKILL
[Design No. 66]

THIS type I made specifically for use in an edition of
Rip Van Winkle which I was making for The Limited Editions Club. As to its inspiration, I have not
the slightest recollection; what I had in mind was
merely to design a type "as simple, legible, vigorous,
clear and effective in detail as I could, and which
would at the same time show no note of strangeness
in the mass." I feel that Kaatskill owes nothing in
its design to any existing face, and the type therefore
is as truly an American type as anything so hidebound by tradition as type can be. In the publisher's
note in this edition of *Rip Van Winkle* I said—
borrowing a phrase from the author's prefatory note
to *Rip Van Winkle* in the first edition of *The Sketch*

A B C D E F G H I J K L M N O
P Q R S T U V W X Y Z & A B C D
E F G H I J K L M N O P Q R S T U V W X Y Z &
a b c d e f g h i j k l m n o p q r s t
u v w x y z ct fi ff ffi fl ffl . , '; : ! ? -
1 2 3 4 5 6 7 8 9 0

Speaking of earlier types, Goudy says :
The old fellows stole all of our best ideas.

Book—"the type itself is not a whit better than it should be."

The type has an added interest in the fact that it was designed, cut, and set in the immediate vicinage of Irving's story—in the foothills of Rip's own Kaatskill mountains, at Marlborough-on-the-Hudson, on my own premises which are said to have been part of the land whereon "Wolfert's Roost" was located.

To execute a commission to print for the Carteret Book Club "a transcript of the diary of an Essex County Maid during the Revolutionary War," I cut the 12-point size and added the long ſ and ligatures which the copy called for; also I cut a lower-case superior "e" from the same "e" pattern used for the "e's" in the text.

REMINGTON TYPEWRITER
[Design No. 67]

TYPEWRITER faces have become so highly conventional that any departure from the usual forms catches the eye unpleasantly. Since each letter occupies the end of a steel punch of fixed width, variable widths, such as are usual in printers' types, is practically impossible. It is difficult to make a lower-case i or m, or a capital I or M, of the same width. As a matter of fact we have become so accustomed to the spacing and shapes of typewriter letters that to make them approximate printers' type, either in shapes or spacing, is to make them strange, and curiously enough, less legible. The Oliver Typewriter some years ago made a face called "print-type," with the forms of each character more like printers' letters than usual, but the result was not entirely successful.

My problem then in making this typewriter alphabet was to attempt a letter that at most I hoped might minimize the appearance of uneven spacing in typewritten matter. This I did by giving my letters a slightly italic effect, which permitted more freedom in details than a pure roman. I could lengthen the serifs of the narrow letters more nearly to fill the "body" and shorten them for the wider characters, and in this way even up somewhat the awkward gaps or crowding between them and their immediate neighbors.

I made a trip to the Remington factory at Ilion, New York, to talk with the Superintendent, to whom I had a note from the President of the Company;

but I found the Superintendent rather antagonistic—
"they didn't need any outsider to make types for
them." I therefore made my own patterns, cut some
matrices, and pulled a proof which is reproduced
herein. I presume the face was put on the typewriter
—Remington paid me well for the design—but I do
not recall ever seeing a letter written in it. I believe
the Monotype cut a machine face from it (without
my permission) for a customer.

Dear Sir —

See remingtn type de
interesting, made at Deepdene
is started. May yet master di
men and shame strangers, enter
demented mangy tramps and rip
stepsister may grasp this, a m
aiming at imaginary enterpris

As this chronicle is partly autobiographical, I would like to include here some incidents that bear a sort of relation to my work as a type designer and founder.

Some years before I began my own letter-cutting, I had in London come across the firm of Bannerman & Son, printers' engineers, who made and sold all sorts of gadgets for typefounders' use—gauges, casters, etc.—and I had bought from them a number of useful items which are not obtainable here because our typefounders and composing-machine manufacturers have adequate machine shops and are themselves able to make such things when they require them. At Bannerman's I had seen a description of a matrix-engraving machine made in Germany. When I was about to start my own letter-cutting, I remembered this machine, and decided I would go over and try to obtain one for my own little shop.

I mentioned my proposed trip on a visit to my printer friend Coggeshall in Utica a few weeks before sailing, and he decided that he and Mrs. Coggeshall would go too; and a few days later George Trenholm, the Boston designer, said he would also like to join the party. The thirty-second anniversary of my marriage to Bertha fell while we were on our way to England; Coggeshall and Trenholm secretly hunted out the ship's printer and concocted a special dinner menu to celebrate the occasion!

A few days before my departure I had received a cablegram from an old friend in London, to whom I had written of my impending visit, asking if I would speak at a meeting of advertising clubs to be held soon after my arrival. To this request I had cabled my acceptance, though I didn't have too much time to get material together for an address. On reaching London, I was surprised to find that the luncheon meeting was scheduled for the following day, was to be in my honor, and—wonder of wonders!—was to be held in the Great Hall of the Worshipful Company of Stationers, to which the leading printers and advertising men from all over England and Scotland had been invited so they might see for themselves what a foreign type-designer looked like.

Percy Gossop, the friend to whom I had written, called for me with a taxi; and when we entered the impressive old building I was amazed (and terrified) at the crowd awaiting me. Among the guests I was delighted to find my old friend Amos Stote, who had carried out a considerable part of the arrangements for the meeting; Bruce Rogers, our fellow-Typophile; the late beloved Burton Emmett; "Steve" Horgan, George F. Trenholm, and many English printers whom I previously had met. I was delighted to see again George W. Jones of Gough Square, who during a visit to New York, at a meeting of the American Institute of Graphic Arts, had said: "Fred Goudy has never done any harm to typography!" I was introduced to the meeting by Sir Ernest Benn, the publisher.

The occasion to me was a memorable one. It is not often that a simple craftsman is so signally honored as to be invited as a guest speaker within the walls of this historic Hall. Examinations in the printing industry are held there, and prizes and certificates of merit are awarded; but these are for

British printers. As I review my talk at this meeting I wish it might have been a more scholarly address, and so more worthy of the occasion. Afterwards there was quite a bit of newspaper publicity on the affair; and my talk was printed, with a portrait, in one of the advertising magazines.

I have somewhere (if they did not burn in 1939) a number of letters from important people who "regretted their inability to be present"—people like His Grace the Archbishop of Canterbury, a Patron of the Worshipful Company, who had a conference at Lambeth Palace, and Gordon Selfridge, proprietor of the great department store (and whom I knew in Chicago), who was on the Continent at the time.

After a few weeks' sightseeing in London, Bertha and I went to Munich, Nuremburg, Frankfort A.M., Offenbach, Mainz and Cologne; and then home by way of Paris. At Frankfort we were the guests of the great Stempel foundry, whose proprietors were very kind. I enjoyed talking there (through an interpreter) to Gustav Mori, a fine, fatherly old gentleman. Then Dr. Klingspor of the Klingspor foundry sent a car to bring us to Offenbach. We enjoyed the visit to this foundry too, where I had hoped to meet and talk with Rudolf Koch, whose work I admire so much, but who was away on a holiday.

Back in Frankfort young Mr. Cunz, nephew of a director of the Stempel foundry, who had at one time visited us at Deepdene, took me to the office of the engraving-machine manufacturer—makers of the machine used at Stempel's and which I had seen in operation. I arranged to buy one, and in due time it reached the Village Letter Foundry.

INSCRIPTION GREEK
[Design No. 68]

I HAD always wanted to do a Greek type—why, I can't say, for if there is anything I know less about than Greek, I can't think of it at the moment. One day, in looking over some reproductions of early stone inscriptions in Greek capitals, I was struck with the number of characters which were exactly like our roman forms, and on counting found that only eleven letters differed from them. The particular inscriptions I was examining were printed in roman small caps with Greek letters to match in size and color, and I decided to design and add these eleven letters to my Kennerley small capitals in the 18-point No. 2 size. In this way I produced a new Greek type. For my printed specimen of the type I copied one of the inscriptions from *Inscriptiones Antiquae*, by Jani Gruteri, 1603, but what it says I have no idea.

The drawings, patterns, matrices and type were lost in the fire.

Some twenty-odd years ago I made a broadside of the Hippocratic Oath, in Forum capitals, which has been highly spoken of. Now, if I am spared long enough, I hope to do a triptych of the Oath in the original Greek, with Latin and English translations, in types made for the purpose.

ΦΙΛΗΣ ΤΟ ΛΑΜΠΡΟΝ ΚΑΙ ΣΟΦΟΝ
ΛΟΥΣ ΤΟ ΤΕΡΓΝΟΝ ΣΧΗΜΑΤΟΣ
ΔΩΝ Η ΒΛΗΖΟΥΣΑ.

TRAJAN TITLE
[Design No. 69]

For The Limited Editions Club's *Rip Van Winkle* title-page I designed a letter for the principal line based on the classic lapidary letters of ancient Rome. After the book was printed, I received a commission to plan a list of the subscribers to the building of the Community House in my old home town of Forest Hills Gardens, Long Island, to be framed and hung on the wall of the house. The chairman of the committee in charge of the work told me there would be something like a thousand names included. I had decided in my own mind that the letters I had made for the words "Rip Van Winkle" on the title-page mentioned would lend themselves to such a use, and I thereupon completed drawings for the remaining letters of the alphabet and made working patterns for cutting matrices.

As a framed list about three feet by five was wanted, I made a calculation as to the size of type I would need, and decided that 18-point would be as large a face as could be used for so many names in

A B C D E F G H I J K L M N O
P Q Q R S T U V W X Y Z &
1 2 3 4 5 6 7 8 9 0 . , ' -

FWG SAYS THE OLD FELLOWS
STOLE ALL OF OUR BEST IDEAS

the size of frame suggested. By the time I had finished cutting the patterns and matrices for the 18-point type, copy for the names came in and I found that the committee had over-estimated the number of names to be shown, and that there were instead something like eight hundred. My 18-point then was too small for the purpose, so I immediately cut the 24-point, and the 48-point to use for the heading letters. As no handmade paper, which I wished to use, was available in so large a sheet as three by five feet, I printed the names in alphabetical order on nine sheets of some fine Italian handmade, and these sheets I later joined to make one large sheet of the right size.

Trajan Title is one of my favorite designs and it has been widely used. I cut it in seven sizes, from 12- to 48-point. It is based on the letters of the inscription at the base of the Trajan column at Rome, erected about 114 A.D., but the letters have not been slavishly copied—the letters are primal.

The English Monotype Company owns the English and Continental rights to the face.

SANS SERIF LIGHT
[Design No. 70]

EVERYTHING said earlier regarding Design No. 65 applies equally to this face, which is a lighter-weight version of No. 65 with only such changes as were necessitated by the change in weight.

AABCDEFGHIJKLMNOPQ
RRSSTTUVWXYZ&.,';:!?-
aabcdeefghijklmnopqrstu
vwxyzfifffffiflffl$1234567890

Speaking of earlier types,
Goudy says: The old fellows
stole all of our best ideas.

MEDIAEVAL
[Design No. 71]

I COME now to what I personally consider one of my most original designs, a letter based on a twelfth-century South German manuscript hand; and my drawings, I believe, present features never before shown in a printer's type. When books were entirely written out by hand they had qualities that made their texts charming which almost always elude successful imitations in metal types. I believe that in the Mediaeval face I really made a contribution to the art and craft of the type founder. Of it I said (pompously) at the time of its making: "if it were to be judged by pragmatic standards it probably would not meet the approval of those critics who demand in their types the elimination of any atavistic tendency. Quite obviously, then, it cannot be judged fairly by the advertising compositor or the job printer."

Mediaeval, in its lower-case, borrows the free-

A B C D E G F F G G H I J K L M N
O P Q R S S T U V W X Y Z & . , ' ; : ! ? '
a b c d e f g h i j k l m n o p q r s t u v w x y z
fi ff ffi fl ffl ll ct æ œ $ 1 2 3 4 5 6 7 8 9 0

Speaking of earlier types, Goudy says:
The old fellows stole all of our best ideas.

dom of the scribe's pen of the Renaissance; its capitals, however, owe less to the pen hands since they are more or less composites of monastic manuscript and Lombardic painted forms. The faint unfamiliarity of some of the characters should prove no bar to its use in texts whose appearance in the printed page need not be sacrificed on the altar of that unknown god "legibility." I did not attempt to sacrifice clearness or significance of the forms themselves in my endeavor to retain some quality of pen work, but I did attempt to secure *in metal* the characteristic handling of the quill; I did not attempt to eliminate the gothic spirit of the face while romanizing somewhat the individual characters of the font. Its final form was essentially the vision of the printer and designer, rather than of the calligrapher.

The new face attracted little general comment; a fact I didn't mind since I sold more of it than many other types in my specimen—so some printers must have liked it. I would like to recut it if there were time, before I enter the shadow.

The University of California Press has used it largely and well; Howard Coggeshall of Utica swears by it. My friend Douglas Barnes had enlargements of it made for his business name with letters cut out of metal—aluminum, I think— for attaching to his show windows in Manhasset, Long Island.

Arthur Rushmore selected Mediaeval for Harper's edition of *Sonnets from the Portuguese* and it made a handsome volume. I first used it for an insert I arranged for *The Colophon* on the "Devices of the Early Italian Printers." The design was begun on August 19, and type cast September 27, 1930.

HADRIANO LOWER-CASE
[Design No. 71A]

This year, 1930, was a fairly prolific one in my type-founding work—seven new types and the lower-case for the Hadriano capitals made in 1918—a record in which I take considerable pride. True, one of them, the Inscription Greek, was not an important addition to my list; but Trajan Title, Sans Serif Light, Mediaeval, Advertiser's Modern, Goudy Stout and Truesdell required a great deal of work for one pair of hands to draw, to cut patterns, and to engrave the matrices.

Hadriano lower-case was made at the request of the Monotype Company which has the reproduction rights for Hadriano. I did not want to attempt a lower-case for a purely inscriptional letter, but the foundries and composing machine companies say printers ask for lower-case regardless of the esthetics of the matter, and I allowed myself to be persuaded.

This design hardly justifies a separate listing herein and is included as a mere matter of record, and date of its making; it might properly have had mention

Here are Letters mamemgh hmimmmpmrmsmtm Eggs Camera Fame Gist Merit it Ragime Dare Pirate Thirst Nights map parts sights are under No. 33, although drawn twelve years later than the capitals which were intended, like my Forum, to stand alone as an inscriptional face.

I made what I thought was a good companion for the capitals, but the first proof disappointed me. The type looked entirely too much like Kennerley Bold (No. 48, done in 1924). I cut one size only and turned the type over to the Monotype. I do not think anything was ever done with it—praise be!

ADVERTISER'S MODERN
[Design No. 72]

I DO not recall at the moment why I began the design for this face, of which nothing remains except a proof of three lines of type I cut and cast for my friend Manuel Rosenberg, editor and publisher of *The Advertiser*, for his yearly *Sketch Book*. This type was sent to the Lakeside Press in Chicago, where the printing of the *Sketch Book* for "Rosie" was being done, for use on the cover. The specimen shown here is a line-cut reproduction of a proof I recently found among odds and ends of remainders of my fire in '39. I do not remember whether all the patterns were made or not; but my recollection is that all of the master patterns had been cut, so all of the drawings must also have been completed.

The Advertiser's SKETCH BOOK 1937

GOUDY STOUT
[Design No. 73]

IN A moment of typographic weakness I attempted to produce a "black" letter that would interest those advertisers who like the bizarre in their print. It was not the sort of a letter I cared for, but requests from some advertisers who saw the first drawings induced me to cut one size and try out the effect. I never cut any but the one size, although I threatened to cut other sizes if any were demanded. None were!

ABCDEFG
HIJKLM
NOPQRST
UVWXYZ
G & . , -

TRUESDELL

THIS face, designed in 1930, was cut in February, 1931. The publishers of *The Colophon, A Book Collectors' Quarterly*, had asked me to contribute a section for No. 5 and I had selected an article on "The Devices of the Early Italian Printers," from Ongania's book on the Italian printers, published by Charles Scribner's Sons and reprinted with their permission. For this reprint, which was in my new Mediaeval—almost its first use—I wrote a prefatory "Note on the Marks of the Early Italian Printers," which I set up in 18-point Kaatskill. As I was allowed two pages only for my note, I soon found that my matter was too long to go in 18-point

A B C D E F G H I J K L M N O P
Q R S T U V W X Y Z & . , ' ; : ! ? -
a b c d e f g h i j k l m n o p q r s t u
v w x y z fi ff ffi fl ffl æ ct st ¶ ([
1 2 3 4 5 6 7 8 9 0

Speaking of earlier types, Goudy says:
The old fellows stole all of our best
ideas.

Kaatskill. Remembering my Truesdell letter, I hurriedly finished the patterns for it and cut and cast a 16-point size (later casting it on an 18-point body), and this 16-point size exactly filled my allotted space.

Of Truesdell, at the time of its making, I said "it is a new face presenting a handling of some details not hitherto shown in any type face." It is an original design in which the capitals follow more or less the pen-drawn letters of the early scribes, but with no loss of the Latin character required in our present-day types. The lower-case letters also show something of the scribes' handling where it occurs naturally, but not to the same extent as in the caps.

I gave the face the name "Truesdell," which was my mother's maiden name.

I have had more orders for Truesdell *since* the fire than before that catastrophe; these latter orders, of course, could not be filled.

TRUESDELL ITALIC
[Design No. 75]

OF this italic, made to accompany the preceding
face, there is little to be said of its origin—it speaks
for itself. Truesdell Italic presents no bizarre or
freakish details and like the Aldine letter will stand
alone. A few details of handling are unusual, but
they merely add interest and do not detract from its
legibility or possible beauty.

Ellen Glasgow wrote me of Truesdell Italic, in
which Earl Emmons had printed "an appreciation"
of her by James Branch Cabell, that it "is a most
beautiful type and I am proud it should distinguish
me in Mr. Emmons's interesting and artistic work."

A B C D E F G H I J K L M N O P
Q R S T U V W X Y Z & A B C
D E G K L P R T U W Y Th

a b c d e f g h i j k l m n o p q r s t u v
w x y z v y fi ff fl ffl ct st . , ' ; : ! ? -

Speaking of earlier types, Goudy says:
The old fellows stole all of our best ideas.

DEEPDENE OPEN TEXT
[Design No. 76]

WHEN my friend Edwin G. Gress, former editor of *The American Printer*, was preparing his book *Fashions in American Typography*, to be published by Harper's, he asked me to write an introduction for it and to suggest a type to use for chapter headings which would harmonize with my Deepdene, which he intended to use for the text matter. I said I would design a letter and cut mats for the chapter headings.

I used the lettering I had drawn for my magazine *Ars Typographica* title and head lines; I made patterns and cut mats, opening up the letters with a white line, and using a Lombardic form of capital. There were more letters required for his work than I anticipated, or I might not have been so free with my promise; but I went ahead with the face, cutting the entire alphabet, although for the purposes of his book b, g, j, k, m, v, y, and z were not needed. I named the face "Deepdene Open Text." I later cut matrices for the same face with the white line of the letters filled in solid and called it Deepdene Text.

This proof shows a new open text in 24 point now in process of cutting It is suited for printing where a touch less austere is wanted than simpler type would allow These characters are set in a face of similar design for use if more color is desired

DEEPDENE TEXT
[Design No. 76A]

THE specimen lines herewith tell the story of this
letter. It is merely the open Deepdene Text in solid
line. I am sorry I did not design special capitals, in
addition to the Lombardic forms, at the time of its
making.

In the best books men talk to
to us their most precious tho
pour their souls into ours. Th
for books! They are the wor

ORNATE TITLE
[Design No. 77]

I CAN'T think of anything special to say about Ornate
Title. It is a simple, decorative face that has been
used by some good presses for use on title-pages
where size of type was more important than blackness of line. Albert Schiller used it successfully for an
advertising customer, but then, Albert always was
trying stunts! The Eucalyptus Press at Mills College,
California, has used it very successfully in several of
its publications. What I have said earlier (page 24)
regarding the letters I did for the Sunday School
room *may be* responsible for the idea of the face.

ABCDEFGHIJ

KLMNOPQRS

TUVWXYZ&.,'-

PRECIOUS

SANS SERIF LIGHT ITALIC
[Design No. 78]

THIS design was made to accompany Design No. 70. I cut the matrices for one size and sent the type to the Monotype Company for reproduction. I have always felt that a sans-serif needed no italic and that to provide one could be only an incongruous addition. I fear it never became very popular.

AABCDEFGHIJKLMMNN
OPQRSTUVWXYZ&.,';:!?-
abcdefghijklmnopqrstuv
wxyzfifffflflffl$1234567890

Speaking of earlier types,
Goudy says: The old fellows
stole all of our best ideas.

DEEPDENE MEDIUM
[Design No. 79]

THERE is not much I can say about this design. It is merely a heavier form of Deepdene for which I cut one size, and sent casts to the Monotype Company for whom it was made. I have never seen any reproductions of it and do not think it was ever put on the market.

ABCDEFGHIJKLMNO
PQRSTUVWXYZ&
abcdefghijklmnopqrstuv
wxyzfiflffffiffl

GOETHE and GOETHE ITALIC
[Designs No. 80 and No. 89]

GOUDY GOETHE is, in the main, a lighter version, with slight changes and refinements, of Goudy Modern (Design No. 35). It was drawn and cut specially to print a specimen I contributed, at the request of Hugo Steiner-Prag, to the Goethe Centenary Exhibition held in Leipzic in 1932. Each contribution presented something from the writings of Goethe, and was printed in the language of the printer. About one hundred printers in various countries of the world (four from the United States) were invited to contribute. For my contribution I printed by hand twelve sheets of a conversation of Goethe with Johann Peter Eckermann on "Literary Style."

In addition to the roman I cut also the italics for one word (*reasons*), later completing the italic alphabet for use in the Limited Editions Club edition of

A B C D E F G H I J K L M N O
P Q R S T U V W X Y Z & . , ' : ; ! ? -
a b c d e f g h i j k l m n o p q r s t u v w x
y z fi ff fl ffi ffl æ 1 2 3 4 5 6 7 8 9 0

Speaking of earlier types, Goudy says:
The old fellows stole all of our best ideas.

Frankenstein, for which I had cut the 12- and 14-point sizes of the roman specially. Bertha did the hand composition of that book (some 300 pages)—the last work she was able to do before her death in 1935.

Of the type, Paul A. Bennett in *The Dolphin*, No. 2, says: "Like Goudy Modern, its heavier inspiration, Goethe is a blending of modern and old style characteristics which, in this instance, produces a distinctively new result. Goethe is unlike any transitional face in its narrow letter forms, yet it has a reading ease superior to that of any strictly modern letter."

I had hoped later to make a new face of this letter by adding a very slight extra weight, with a few other revisions also, but never got beyond making a few sketches to remind me of my intention; these sketches burned in 1939.

A B C D E F G H I J K L M N O P

Q R S T U V W X Y Z & . , ' ; : ! ? -

a b c d e f g h i j k l m n o p q r s t u v w

x y z fi fl ff ffi Th ä ô 1 2 3 4 5 6 7 8 9 0

Speaking of earlier types, Goudy says :
The old fellows stole all of our best ideas.

FRANCISCAN
[Design No. 81]

FRANCISCAN is the name given by Edwin Grabhorn to the *redesigned and recut* Aries face (Design No. 54). Grabhorn had purchased the face after seeing a proof of it on the occasion of my visit to his shop in San Francisco in 1931. I had renamed the Aries face "Village Text," and intended to use it for my own printing rather than to offer it for general sale.

Grabhorn first used it for printing *The Spanish Occupation of California*, in February 1934. This book took highest honors at the American Institute of Graphic Arts "Fifty Books of the Year" exhibition that year. It was also used to print the Grabhorn Press *Bibliography*, in 1940. I am not sure in my own mind that this type was the best that might have been selected for this bibliography, even though it was my design and the property of the Press; but

A B C D E G F G H I J K L M N
O O D Q R S T U V W X Y Z ℘
& & . : ; / ? ! ' 1 2 3 4 5 6 7 8 9 0
a b c d e f g h i j k l m n o p q r s t u v
w x y z ff fi fl ffi ffl ct
Speaking of earlier types, Goudy says:
The old fellows stole all of our best ideas.

I believe it to be well adapted for reprints of matter leaning toward the archaic. In Grabhorn's use of it for the Book Club of California's folio about the first edition of the King James Bible, with a genuine 1611 leaf included, I can find no fault. The type adapts itself beautifully to a two-column page.

The matrices were electrotyped by the Monotype Company from my redesigned types and cast for Grabhorn by McKenzie and Harris, San Francisco.

DEEPDENE BOLD
[Design No. 82]

THIS design was projected about the time of my talks with William Edwin Rudge regarding his proposal to buy Deepdene, which I have related earlier under the heading for Design No. 58. This transaction falling through, the actual drawings were postponed until after the Monotype Company had produced Deepdene and Italics.

For this face I cut one size and sent the type to the Company for weight, fitting, etc. Until a few weeks ago (September, 1944) I was not aware that the face had been reproduced. Recently I received some sheets showing Deepdene Bold from 6-point to 72-point.

Of it Monotype publicity says, "this face was created by F. W. Goudy as a bold companion for his Deepdene series. Like its companion face the design is clean-cut and legible. It is bold without offensive blackness."

ABCDEFGHIJKLMNOP
QRSTUVWXYZ&.,';:!?-
abcdefghijklmnopqrstuvw
xyzfifffffflflffl$1234567890

Speaking of earlier types,
Goudy says: The old fellows
stole all of our best ideas.

MOSTERT
[Design No. 83]

THERE is little to say about this face, as nothing remains to substantiate any statement I might make. I had, at the request of my friend Paul B. Hoeber, the medical book publisher, bought from him a *handwritten* book, which had been consigned to him for possible sale. It had been written by Annelise Mostert, Stuttgart (Germany) in 1923, on Locke's *Causes of Weakness in Men's Understandings*. The writing was well done in a pseudo-roman letter presenting an interesting page, and to recoup the cost of the book I used it as a basis for a type.

Drawings were made and the lower-case and some capitals cut, but the few proofs pulled indicated that the type would hardly be worth going on with, as the printed page seemed to have lost every quality that had made the handwritten pages interesting. Therefore nothing further was done and drawings and matrices burned in 1939. The book I used as a model for my type is among my books in the Library of Congress.

VILLAGE No. 2

EVER since the time I sold the matrices and design
for the original Village type, with which the Village
Press had started in 1903, to Frederick Sherman,
I had wanted something to replace it—not to imitate it, but rather to have something of similar
weight and adapted to similar uses. The original
Village type showed some features which I would
discard and I wished to make the new type as simple
and as free from any flamboyant features as possible.
I think the first use I made of it was to reprint an
article "The Old and The New" by Theodore L.
DeVinne, that had appeared in *The Book-lover's
Almanac* for 1898. My reprint in the 14-point size
was made in June 1933.

Mr. Best of the Monotype Company asked for
the reproduction rights. It was put on the machine
in 14- and 18-point composition, but owing to

A B C D E F G H I J K L M N O P

Q R S T U V W X Y Z & A B C D E

F G H I J K L M N O P Q R S T U V W X Y Z

a b c d e f g h i j k l m n o p q r s t u v

w x y z fi ff ffi fl ffl 1 2 3 4 5 6 7 8 9 0

Speaking of earlier types, Goudy says :
The old fellows stole all of our best ideas.

differences of opinion as to certain details regarding its reproduction it became the subject of an acrimonious dispute, and I think no other sizes were ever cut by the company. The company did sponsor a finely planned booklet printed by the Haddon Craftsmen, designed by my friend Richard Ellis, to commemorate the presentation to me of the Ulster-Irish Society's medal of honor, at a dinner at the Commodore Hotel in New York in March 1937; the booklet was set in 18-point Village. The presentation of the medal was made by my friend the Hon. Secretary of Labor, Frances Perkins.

I have used the face frequently, notably in my book *Capitals from the Trajan Column at Rome*, and for the book about *The Time Capsule* buried at Flushing Meadows, Queens, New York (location of the World's Fair), not to be resurrected for 5000 years. The Press of the Woolly Whale used it to reprint my essay *Design and Beauty in Printing*, first spoken at the twelfth annual Conference on Printing Education in June, 1933, at Columbia University. This essay was one of the items included in the *Time Capsule*.

To my mind, Village No. 2 is an excellent type.

QUINAN OLD STYLE
[Design No. 85]

HENRY B. QUINAN, art diréctor for the *Woman's Home Companion* (published by the Crowell Company) intimated that *The American Magazine*, also published by Crowell, was thinking of having a new type for its headings. He wouldn't give an order for a letter, but he would consider seriously any design I cared to submit. Ordinarily I would not consider a speculative commission, but my relations with Quinan had been cordial and I figured that I might make something for the magazine which, even if it did not please the publisher, would still be a new type for my own stock. I thereupon made the face which is reproduced herein. But it did not prove bizarre enough to meet the growing tendency among magazines for startling effects that is only now (1943) slowly abating. I planned to complete the cutting and make a few revisions, but never got around to the work. Nothing remains of it except the proof reproduced herewith.

ible to a high degree. In its essen
tial letter forms it presents few
departures from good tradition
although showing a new hand
ling of some features in indivi
THESE ARE THE CAPITALS
OF THE FONT. B D Q F J G &

GOUDY BOLD FACE
[Design No. 86]

THAT this design was made must be accepted as fact by the reader solely on my statement. Why I made it, I can't imagine, unless possibly my list of types didn't at this time include a letter with its weight and character. Unfortunately the drawings, patterns and matrices disappeared in the fire. While working on this chronicle of designs, a proof showed up which I intended to reproduce here and thus substantiate my statement that there was such a design; but when the manuscript was ready for the printer, the proof itself had unaccountably disappeared and diligent search has failed to resurrect it. The proof did not indicate that the type would have proved much of an addition to my stock of types, except by way of variety.

As this account of my types is a record of work performed, my opinion regarding their excellences, or lack of them, is incidental, and not the primary reason for the inclusion of such designs as the one above mentioned; they are included merely to make the record complete. (Since this account was put in type, the proof referred to has turned up and is shown herein.)

ABCEPNOTRmbdh
norspufvylg'-,.iaetc

For the types numbered 87, 88, 95, 96, 98, 99, 102, 103 and 104 in *The Record of Goudy Types* prepared by Earl Emmons and myself and "presented by the late Dave Gildea as a memento for visitors at the Celebration of the Thirty-fifth Anniversary of the Village Press, held at Deepdene, Marlboro, New York, July 23, 1938," absolutely nothing remains after the fire either in proof or in my recollection. That such drawings and sketches existed there is no doubt, as Emmons and I went over the drawings themselves carefully and for some of them which at that time (just prior to the celebration) were as yet without identifying names, we selected names which later could be changed if desirable. Even the names bring nothing definite to my mind as to the character of any of them—as far as they are concerned my mind is a blank. The designs as we named them were: Goudy Book, Hudson, Textbook Old Style, Hasbrouck, Atlantis, Millvale, Mercury, and sketches for two unnamed. *

Evidently the year 1933 passed with practically nothing to show as to new designs, unless, as is probable, some of the lost items listed in *The Record of Goudy Types* were done that year. The few records that were saved from the 1939 fire do not disclose any information as to dates.

*These names sound as though copied from Pullman sleepers!

DEEPDENE BOLD ITALIC
[Design No. 90*]

THE Deepdene Bold Italic drawings gave me more trouble than any italic I had hitherto attempted. I finally scrapped all of my preliminary sketches and began a design that would not be merely a heavier facsimile of the italic Deepdene, since I had come to believe that a bold letter can do little more than approximate in form the roman it is to complement —the additional weight or color can be added only set-wise: the lower-case x height remains unchanged. Therefore my thought was merely to make my new italic bear the same relation of weight to

A B C D E F G H I J K L M N O P
Q R S T U V W X Y Z & . , ' ; : ! ?
a b c d e f g h i j k l m n o p q r s t u v w
x y z fi ff ffi fl ffl $ 1 2 3 4 5 6 7 8 9 0

Speaking of earlier types,
Goudy says: The old fellows
stole all of our best ideas.

*At the time I was preparing my notes for Deepdene Bold and Deepdene Bold Italic, I was not aware that the Monotype Company had reproduced Deepdene Bold Italic and I had not expected to be able to exhibit a specimen. I now find (September, 1944) it has been made in the same point sizes as its companion face, 6- to 12-point in composition and 14- to 72-point for handsetting.

the Deepdene Bold already drawn, as the Deepdene Italic bears to the Deepdene roman; keeping in mind, of course, its general form and idiosyncrasies of handling.

The Monotype showing of the face says "in placing crispness into Deepdene Bold Italic, Mr. Goudy has maintained in it the outstanding features of his other Deepdene faces . . . The inclination is somewhat less than is usual in italic designs, and the letters have a pen-drawn effect which is distinctive as well as pleasing. The Deepdene family is unique among Mr. Goudy's diversified types."

SAKS GOUDY and ITALIC
[Designs No. 91 and No. 92]

IT gave me great pleasure when I received a request from the Saks Fifth-Avenue advertising manager, Mrs. Moser, for some information as to what steps for them to take to acquire a type for the exclusive use of that great store. Calling at an early opportunity I went over the ground with Mrs. Moser as to the number of sizes that might be wished, both in roman and italic; whether I would be asked also to furnish the cast type; the cost of design—in short, all the details of the possible order.

She introduced me to Adam Gimbel, the manager of the store a most charming and cultured gentleman and a much younger man than I had expected to see. He was very much interested in my work—in fact he seemed to be more interested in that than in the matter in hand, which he practically left to Mrs. Moser to take care of.

In the course of a day or two I wrote her a letter, giving a price for the design, reciting the details we had discussed, and the probable time required to do the work. In a day or two I received the order to go ahead and a check enclosed on account as an earnest of payment. Thus began one of the pleasantest and most satisfactory business transactions of my whole type-founding career.

I did not show any drawings to Mrs. Moser but began cutting matrices for the 24-point size as soon as I had finished my drawings. A proof was pulled and I felt like saying, as William Morris said when he first saw the copy of his monumental Chaucer,

"My eyes! how good it is!" Evidently Mrs. Moser and Mr. Gimbel also thought it was good, for I was instructed to proceed with the work.

In the fall of 1934, Saks Fifth-Avenue staged a show of my work, featuring their design, at the National Arts Club. There was a big crowd on the

ABCDEFGHIJKLMNOP
QRSTUVWXYZ&.,';:!?ʾ

ABCDEFGHIJKLMNOPQRSTUVWXYZ&

abcdefghijklmnopqrstuvw
xyz fi ff ffi fl ffl & 1234567890
Of earlier types, FWG says: The
old fellows stole our best ideas.

ABCDEFGHIJKLMNOPQ
RSTUVWXYZ&.,';:!?ʾ
abcdefghijklmnopqrstuvwxyz
ABCDEGPRT fi ff ffi fl ffl ft &
Speaking of earlier types, Goudy says:
The old fellows stole all of our best ideas.

opening night. I was the guest at a dinner given me at Hotel Lafayette by Mr. and Mrs. Adam Gimbel preceding the opening. The late Pirie McDonald, the men's photographer on Fifth Avenue, put a large portrait he had made of me in his street show-case with a printed card calling attention to the National Arts Show (set in a type not mine, of course).

I believe that Saks Goudy is as good a type as I have ever made, or can make; and that the Italic is one of the best italics I've ever done, although my University of California Old Style Italic probably is its equal.

One day Mrs. Moser, at my invitation, came out to my shop where I was engraving Saks matrices. She watched the process with a great deal of interest. She asked what metal I was engraving and jokingly I said "Gold." For a moment she believed me, as I was using polished brass blocks which did look like gold. Her inquiry however gave me an idea, and I suggested actually cutting a matrix in gold—a thing I didn't believe had ever been done; and a few days later along came a little bar of 10-carat gold about a quarter of an inch thick, three-eighths of an inch wide, and about an inch and three-quarters long. I started engraving a cap italic "G" and my troubles began. Gold is a "sticky" metal; it tears rather than cuts (perhaps because I was not using a cutting tool best adapted to cutting it) and I broke some five or six tools before finally getting a satisfactory matrix. This matrix, with a description of it and a proof, was exhibited at the National Arts Club. It is now in the Library of Vassar College, the gift of Saks Fifth-Avenue.

In addition to the normal Saks roman and italic, I used my patterns for the small caps to cut matrices the height of the capitals, thus producing some "bold" caps for display lines. I don't remember how many sizes were cut.

[Design No. 92A]

ABCDEFGHIJKLMNO
PQRSTUVWXYZ&.,'⁓
FWG SAYS: THE OLD
FELLOWS STOLE ALL

In the list of my types printed for the celebration of the 35th anniversary of the Village Press the type numbered 93 (Cloister Initials) was chronologically misplaced, and therefore incorrectly numbered. In the present record that type has been properly placed and given its correct date, 1918. To avoid changing all the numbers following No. 31, it has been given the intermediate number 31A. As Hadriano Stone Cut was made about this date (1934) it has been given the number formerly given incorrectly to Cloister Initials.

HADRIANO STONE CUT
[Design No. 93]

ON THE occasion of one of my frequent visits to the
Monotype offices in Philadelphia I found that the
company (without previous consultation with me)
had tried the experiment of cutting a white line
through each of the letters of my Hadriano. The
idea, I regret, had not occurred to me, but a proof of
the changed letters pleased me so much that I immediately gave permission to issue matrices of the
characters for general sale.

Hadriano Stone Cut is not, in a strict sense, a new
design, but its appearance more nearly approximates
the spirit of the original inscription and presents
such a new expression that I feel it deserves a mention and exhibition in this record.

A B C D E F G H I J
K L M N O P Q R S
T U V W X Y Z &
1 2 3 4 5 6 7 8 9 0 . , ´

VILLAGE ITALIC
[Design No. 94]

THIS italic was made, of course, to accompany Village No. 2 (Design No. 84) and the specimen shows a simple, straightforward design with no special features to speak of.

A B C D E F G H I J K L M N O P
Q R S T U V W X Y Z & a b c d e f g
h i j k l m n o p q r s t u v w x y z ct st ff ffl

Speaking of earlier types, Goudy says:
The old fellows stole all of our best ideas.

TORY TEXT
[Design No. 97]

I HAD the intention of printing a small edition of
Aucassin et Nicolette, the Twelfth Century love
story, with facing pages of an English translation on
one page with the old French version on the facing
page. I have Andrew Lang's delightful translation
which I planned to use for copy. I felt that a type
which would reflect, in a way, the spirit of the
ancient *cante-fable* would be desirable; and the
"lettres batarde" shown in the Grolier Club edition
of Geofroy Tory's *Champ Fleury* on the correct proportions of letters came to my mind.

Tory's book is said to be "at once the most useless
and the most curious book on lettering in existence."
but nevertheless it gave me, in one of Tory's alphabets, exactly what I wanted—a basic letter which I
could employ to design a new type which would be
useful for reprints of an archaic nature, at least. As I
did not intend merely to present a facsimile of Tory,

𝕬𝕭𝕮𝕯𝕰𝕱𝕲𝕳𝕴𝕵𝕶𝕷𝕸𝕹𝕺𝕻
𝕼𝕽𝕾𝕿𝖀𝖁𝖂𝖃𝖄𝖅 & .,';:!?⸗
abcdefghijklmnopqrstuvwx
yz fi ff ffi fl ffl Th «» 1234567890

Speaking of earlier types, Goudy says:
The old fellows stole all of our best ideas.

I found I had to make a number of departures from his letters, simplifying some of them and redrawing others to meet the elements of legibility needed for us moderns; I attempted to interpret the spirit and *elan* of the old work, rather than to attempt a revival of an old type.

Earl Emmons used Tory Text for a special four-page announcement of the Ulster-Irish Society of New York's presentation to me of their medal of honor, printed on a sheet of "Worthy Book" paper especially watermarked with a portrait of myself.

Tory Text is one of my favorite types and I enjoyed every minute of its making.

BERTHAM
[Design No. 100]

THIS type came about curiously enough through a request by Laurence Siegfried, then editor of *The American Printer*, to contribute an article on my "one hundredth type," which as yet wasn't even started—in fact Numbers 98 and 99 weren't done, either, but I had started drawings for them, doing enough work on each to show my ideas and to receive work numbers. (See paragraph three of the remarks on Design No. 86.)

Shortly before his request I had purchased a book I really couldn't afford, set in a type derived from one used by F. Holle to print Ptolemy's *Geographica* at Ulm in 1482. I didn't think the type in this book was well done, but the color of the page was good and certain features in the letter made me wonder whether I could make a new type suggested by it that might prove successful. I began by idly drawing characters based on the Holle type, and soon became

A B C D E F G H I J K L M N O P
Q R S T U V W X Y Z & . , ' ; : ! ? -
a b c d e f g h i j k l m n o p q r s t u v
w x y z fi ff fl ct st 1 2 3 4 5 6 7 8 9 0

Speaking of earlier types, Goudy says :
The old fellows stole all of our best ideas.

engrossed in the attempt to turn a fifteenth-century type into one for twentieth-century readers.

Just then came the request by Siegfried. This was on May 30, 1936. The article was wanted "next week"—could I draw all of the letters, make eighty patterns to scale, engrave matrices and cast type in time to meet the magazine's deadline? On June 5 I had forty-three characters ready for final revision, and on June 22 the type shown herein was cast, just sixteen working days after its inception.* As I worked, the idea came to me that I might dedicate this "one hundredth type" to my beloved helpmate, Bertha M. Goudy, who had worked with me so unselfishly for so many years, and for a first use of the new type I would print a little tribute to her memory. The type, at first unnamed, I later gave the name "Bertham," by combining her first name and middle initial.

In September, 1936, the Syracuse University School of Journalism used Bertham to print my *Types of the Past*, an address I gave at the New York Press Association Dinner, beautifully printed for the school by Howard Coggeshall. In *Bookmaking on the Distaff Side*, 1937, appeared an article I wrote for it on "Bertha M. Goudy 1869-1935," set by Marie Berliner in Bertham, and printed at the Walpole Printing Office. Later I had this article reprinted in Bertham with an introduction and much additional matter in a memorial to BMG—"by one who knew her best"—at Coggeshall's press.

*I had to be away from the shop for a few days on other matters—which accounts for the apparent inaccuracy as to elapsed time.

"By the fire of 1939 the tools, types, proofs hallowed by the touch of B.M.G.'s consummate craftsmanship have gone forever, save only in poignant memories that will never dim."

Following is the tribute which was written for the first use of Bertham:

A TRIBUTE TO B M G

These lines present my one-hundredth type design before lining, fitting, or final revision. The type, drawn in humility, is dedicated to the memory of my beloved helpmate

BERTHA M. GOUDY

She encouraged me when my own courage faltered; uncomplaining she endured the privations and vicissitudes of our early companionship; her intelligent and ready counsel I welcomed and valued; her consummate craftsmanship made possible many difficult undertakings; she ever sought to minimize any exploitation of her own great attainments, that the acclaim which rightfully was hers should come, instead, to me. For two-score years, in every way, she unselfishly aided me in my work in the fields of type design and typography and enabled me to attain a measure of success which alone I could not have achieved.

F.W.G.

Marlboro, June, 1936

PAX
[Design No. 101]

THE name 'Pax" was one suggested to me at the time of the Ulster-Irish dinner in 1937 for a new type that would somehow or other have to do with the idea of "peace." I don't remember, at the moment, just how it was to come about with a type, but I nevertheless went ahead with a design and made all or nearly all the master patterns. Nothing further was done with it until the matter of a type for the University of California Press came up a year later and the rest of the story about "Pax" is continued in the account of type No. 106.

Designs numbered 102, 103, 104 were sketches for designs more or less complete, but destroyed in the fire. They are listed in the index hereafter since they had been assigned identifying numbers and work had been done on all of them.

FRIAR
[Design No. 105]

FRIAR type was designed for my own amusement, and I had a lot of fun, too, doing it. For the lower-case, I drew on the half-uncial forms of the fourth, fifth and sixth centuries, on eighth-century uncials, on the interesting types of Victor Hammer and Rudolf Koch. For my capitals, I combined letters based on the square capitals of the fourth century, the Rustic hands of the mediaeval scribes—and to all of these suggestions I added my own conceits.

I wanted to do something for a Christmas keepsake, which my friend Coggeshall would print for me—he to retain part of the edition for his own use. He made several suggestions as to subject matter but none of them met my fancy. On September 12 I wrote him "Been busy all week on a new type. Instead of the booklet you propose, why not do the little thing I am inclosing, written by Eugene Field,

A A B C D E E F G H Ꜧ I J K L M N O
P Q R S T T U V W X Y Z & ꜩ ff fl ffl
a a ʙ b b c d ꝺ e e f g ꞇ h i j k l m n o p
q ʀ r s t u v w x y z . , ' ; : ! ? ⁄ · ❦ ✠ ✤

1 2 3 4 5 6 7 8 9 0

Speaking of earlier types, Gouᴅy says:
The olᴅ fellows stole all of our ʙest ideas.

214

called *The Story of St. Gonsol?*'' For the type to be used in printing it I suggested this new type I was working on. My suggestion brought his immediate acceptance, and I hurried on the work of cutting, in 12-point, a type the exact like of which I had never attempted nor had ever seen. The proofs pleased me and I laid out a specimen page for the little St. Gonsol.

Whether anyone else cared for the type was immaterial to me, but I found a number of printers who did like it. Jane Grabhorn of the Colt Press in San Francisco did, and I sent her fifty pounds of it to play with. The New York School of Printing used it to print an address of mine, about the Bible, on the occasion of a gift to the school library, by the Principal, of the great Oxford Lectern Bible printed by Bruce Rogers. Coggeshall found quite a bit of use for it, as he likes it almost as much as I do myself. There probably aren't more than a couple of hundred pounds in existence since the fire.

The St. Gonsol is a delightful story for book lovers. St. Francis, one of the characters in it, was my old friend the late Frank Morris, rare book dealer of Chicago; St. Gonsol was Dr. Frank Gunsaulus, whom I met on one or two occasions; the other was the Evil One himself.* One day a student at Vassar, who had seen a copy in the Library there, wrote me to ask whether I had an extra copy which she could buy to present to her father, who, she said, was the *son* of the St. Francis of the little book. Fortunately I found a copy which I sent her with my compliments, as there were none for sale.

*[No friend of mine.]

UNIVERSITY OF CALIFORNIA
OLD STYLE and ITALIC
[Designs No. 106 and No. 107]

In December, 1936, Samuel T. Farquhar, manager of the University of California Press, wrote me that one of the Regents of the University (Edward Dickson) had suggested to the president that their Press should have its own type face. Farquhar asked whether I would be interested in designing a face for it. This was something I had long wanted to do and I immediately wrote him, "It is a coincidence that your inquiry should follow so closely upon the heels of the practical completion of my one hundred-first type design, a face that I hope may prove the best of its kind in my long list of type faces; and strangely enough it is exactly the type I would make if I had actually had the University in mind while employed on it." This was the design "Pax" I have referred to under No. 101.

However, no definite word regarding a design for the Press came. In April or May, 1937, I decided to take a vacation and go to Los Angeles and Berkeley. While in Los Angeles, Mr. Dickson, the Regent I have mentioned, came to my hotel for a little talk; he kindly took me out to the Clarke Library. We talked over the project of a type and other things typographical and on May 12 he wrote Farquhar regarding the new type he had suggested. Still no definite decision was reached until December 1937, when Farquhar wired me to go ahead with the design and also that he would be in Marlborough about January 15, 1938, to see progress.

I at once began cutting matrices of my No. 101, for which I already had patterns, and by January 8 I was able to pull a proof of a few paragraphs; at sight of it my heart sank—it was one of those disappointments that occasionally come to a designer. It simply would not do.

What to do next? Farquhar was to be here within the week and I must have something to show him. Reluctantly I hid away from the sight of man the drawings and proof of No. 101, and started new drawings, new patterns, new matrices. My! did I work! I went almost without food or sleep, but a proof of the new design was ready to show Farquhar when he arrived. Then I showed him No. 101. He told me afterward that he would have accepted it if I had shown it to him *first*, but not

A B C D E F G H I J K L M N O
P Q R S T U V W X Y Z & . , ’-:;!?

ABCDEFGHIJKLMNOPQRSTUVWXYZ
a b c d e f g h i j k l m n o p q r s t u
v w x y z fi ff ffi fl ffl ct st Æ Œ æ œ
1 2 3 4 5 6 7 8 9 0

Speaking of earlier types, Goudy says: The old fellows stole all of our best ideas.

after seeing the new one. Of the new design I said: "I elected to make a type for general use the desideratum, rather than a type for more sumptuous work." I endeavored to give to it the utmost distinction compatible with its purpose and especially strived for the greatest legibility possible. In short, I tried to create a distinguished type expression in mass which would not violate good tradition, nor be reminscent of other types of mine.

For my italic I wanted to draw a refined letter that could not be called prudish. Some of the characters may be a bit exuberant, but not more so than due regard for its purpose permits.

For the first use of the University of California Old Style Farquhar asked me if I would write and plan a book on the general subject of type design, typography, etc., and in 1939 I forwarded the manuscript for *Typologia*, a book of 170 pages, which later was published by the Press. I went out to Berkeley in the Summer of 1940 and worked with the printers for some weeks.

The book was published with considerable *eclat*

A B C D E F G H I J K L M N O P Q R S
T U V W X Y Z & Æ Œ œ ﬆ ﬅ . ," - ; : ! ?
a b c d e f g h i j k l m n o p q r s t u v w x y z
ﬁ ﬀ ﬂ ﬃ ﬄ A B C D E G M R T g v w

Speaking of earlier types, Goudy says:
The old fellows stole all of our best ideas.

on October 23, 1940, as the contribution by the Press to the celebration of the 500th anniversary of Gutenberg's invention of typography. A large number of friends of the Press, literary people, my own friends, newspaper reporters, members of the faculty of the University, editors and office employees were invited to be present, and all afternoon and evening the rooms of the Press were thronged with an interested lot of visitors. The exercises were simple; Farquhar made a little address, presenting me with copy No. 2 of the "autographed edition of *Typologia*, limited to 300 copies," to which I responded briefly.

The Press has used the letter for several books; its latest important use is in the newly revised and enlarged edition—the sixth—of my combined *Alphabet* and *Elements of Lettering* and the Press recently did a broadside of the "Oath of Hippocrates" in a large size of the roman with the heading in my Goudy Text, which I think is an outstanding example of printing, and a wonderful showing of the face itself.

University of California Old Style is one face for which I have no regrets. One change only in the original design of one character was asked: Farquhar did not like my lower-case "y," so I made a more conventional form for him. These lines are written in 1943—the type is now four years old, and to me it improves with age.

(*In 1959, Lanston Monotype issued this face publicly, with the permission of the University of California, and the name was changed to Californian.—Pub.*)

NEW VILLAGE TEXT
[Design No. 108]

THE Grabhorn Press of San Francisco wrote me that they were going to do a book for the Book Club of California on Caxton, England's first printer; each book was to include a genuine leaf of Caxton's *Polychronicon* of 1482.

The Press ordered a considerable font of my Deepdene Text to use for its composition, but I didn't want to fill the order as I wasn't entirely satisfied in my own mind that this Text was the best type for the work proposed. I studied the matter over quite a bit, and then an inspiration came—and no sooner thought than tried. I had my son cast capitals of my Tory Text (No. 97) in 24-point to line with the

𝔄 𝔅 ℭ 𝔇 𝔈 𝔉 𝔊 ℌ 𝔍 𝔍 𝔎 𝔏 𝔐
𝔑 𝔒 𝔓 𝔔 𝔑 𝔖 𝔗 𝔘 𝔙 𝔚 𝔛
𝔜 𝔷 & 1 2 3 4 5 6 7 8 9 0
❡ a b c d e f g h i j k l m n o p q r
s t u v w x y z ffl ff fl «;:'!?.,'»
Goudy says: The old fellows
stole all of our best ideas.

lower-case of the 24-point Deepdene Text (No. 76A) and I was immediately struck with the Caxton-ish quality exhibited by the proof.

Sending a specimen proof of a paragraph by airmail to Grabhorn, with the request that he substitute the new type, I was gratified a few days later to receive a telegram ordering a considerable quantity of it, and cancelling his previous order.

I planned to make the same combination of Tory Text capitals with the 18-point size of Deepdene Text, but the fire intervened.

I had named Design No. 81 "Village Text," but when Grabhorn bought it he renamed it "Franciscan," leaving me free to use the name "Village Text" for the new face—for the use of the different capitals really made it a new face, the effect was so striking. Of course "Village Text" is not in strict sense a new design; it is simply a composite of two existing designs; but it is nevertheless entitled to a number in these annals because of the new expression it gives in the printed page.

MURCHISON
[Design No. 109]

ONE day early this year I was asked by Mr. Murchison of the Photostat Corporation if I would see him regarding a new type for a composing machine he had invented, or at least in which he was interested. I must confess I never quite understood its possible value to the printing craft, although I grasped fully the principle behind the machine. Its main feature was a round bar or axle for a number of ten-inch wheels; around the perimeter of each wheel was an alphabet of raised letters. By the operation of a knob at one side, the wheels revolved into place and were brought together, so that a line of letters was presented from which to print.

After my talk with Murchison I decided that the simplest form of a sturdy type letter, with no freakish or fanciful features, was all that was called for.

Murchison approved the design I made for him; but when I visited the engravers who were to do the work of translating the drawings into punches, I became convinced that my drawings alone would not be enough, because of the workmen's lack of precision equipment and also because of their lack of experience for such work. Therefore, without consultation with Murchison, and without adding to my original figure for the design itself, I made patterns, cut matrices, and cast type in one size so that the engravers would have something exact as to form and dimensions to work from. Even then I found their final letters were not always good facsimiles, either in form or dimensions.

BULMER
[Design No. 109A]

JUST a few days before the fire in January, 1939, I had, at the request of Mr. Best of the Monotype Company, begun the drawings for a new book type to compete with the "Bulmer" already produced by the type foundries and composing-machine companies.

I have a copy of *Hobbinol* by W. Somerville, a book printed by William Bulmer at the Shakespeare Printing-Office, and published by Ackerman, in 1813. This book, a square quarto, showed two roman types; one, a large face, presented the publisher's "advertisement," and the other, a smaller and quite different face, was used for the preface. The Bulmer types made by the foundries and composing-machine companies ostensibly were modelled on this smaller face. I suggested to Best that to my eye this smaller type lacked wholly the life and variety displayed by the larger, and that a new "Bulmer" following the lines of the more interesting larger face would give the Monotype an opportunity to present a traditional type that would display the same freedom from commonplace reproduction that I had endeavored to give to my drawings of "Garamont" made for the Monotype Company in 1921.

I drew some twenty-odd characters which I submitted to Mr. Best but nothing was done about the design at that time. Later I requested that the drawings be returned to me, and as I look at them today, I realize they failed to carry the quality of freedom and individuality I had hoped to put in them. The drawings may exactly reproduce the *form* of the originals, but there is not in them that intangible something—the spirit or personality of the designer that gives distinction to a type. I hope to take up the drawings again and put into them the spark of life they now lack.

I insert this account here as a matter of record.

SCRIPPS COLLEGE OLD STYLE
[Design No. 110]

My first visit to the Scripps campus in Claremont,
California, was in 1938. I was impressed by the
beautiful library presided over by Dorothy Drake,
the charming Librarian, with whom I became acquainted through Dorothy Bevis, then at Dawson's
Book Shop in Los Angeles. Later visits reinforced
my impressions of the College and all that makes it
a place of delight. When Miss Drake suggested to
the faculty that she would like a type for the use of
those students interested in bookmaking and the arts
of the book, it did not seem then that such a thing
would ever come about. It did later, through the

A B C D E F G H I J K L M N O P

Q R S T U V W X Y Z & . , ' ; : ! ? -

ABCDEFGHIJKLMNOPQRSTUVWXYZ&

a b c d e f g h i j k l m n o p q r s t u v w

x y z fi ff ffi fl ffl ct æ ct 1 2 3 4 5 6 7 8 9 0

Speaking of earlier types, Goudy
says: The old fellows stole all of
our best ideas.

kindness of the late Mrs. Catherine Coffin Phillips, an author (and, I think, a relative of one of the students at Scripps), who made a gift of money for a new type for the Hartley Burr Alexander Press, named for the late instructor of art at Scripps. Not, indeed, enough to cover the cost of design and every detail of necessary expense; but as I was so interested in the project I was impelled to do more for the Press than her money gift would cover.

The type itself is a straightforward, simple design that displays no freakish qualities. It is not "foolproof"—it requires careful handling to bring out its best—but after all, that is what a school press is for, and the work I have seen from the Press indicates an earnest effort on the part of the students to make a good "impression" with the type on the old hand press given to the Press by my friend Ward Ritchie.

Scripps type represents the first matrix cutting I had been able to undertake since the fire. A year or so after the fire, the University of Syracuse had purchased a small equipment for engraving matrices, to be operated by one of the instructors in the School of Journalism. This instructor had had some previous experience in such work and he was to carry on more or less under my direction. But before actually getting at the work for which the equipment was purchased, he resigned to take a position with a commercial house in New York, leaving the equipment with no one to use it.

As the School had no immediate use for the equipment, and knowing that it would be practically impossible for me to acquire it elsewhere because of priority restrictions, the University generously turned it over to me to enable me to carry on my work of matrix engraving.

For my Scripps type I made my large master patterns as I had always made them; but I had no suitable engraving machine for reducing them to the smaller metal working patterns. To engrave such metal work patterns on a machine intended for matrix engraving (a sort of work for which it was not adapted) proved a difficult problem, requiring great care in handling and a much longer time than if the work could have been done on a suitable machine. I wanted to buy such a machine for making patterns but until September 1943 I was unable to get a priority order to do so. Despite the difficulties I did, however, finally cut about 104 16-point matrices, from which I had type cast for the Press by McKenzie & Harris of San Francisco.

GOUDY "THIRTY"
[Design No. 111]

Tʜɪs type (so far under cover and in course of revision to adapt it to the Monotype die case, pattern making, etc.), was begun a year or two ago to submit to a college in the West which was then seeking a type for its Press; but due to war restrictions the commission fell through. When Mr. Best of the Monotype Company suggested that the Company might bring out a type *after I had passed on*, to be called "Goudy Thirty," this design, which I had been working on at odd times, struck me as particularly adapted to the purpose. As I worked on it I had determined to make it, as far as I was able, my last word in type design, a type in which I would give my imagination full rein, and a type by which as a designer I would be willing to stand or fall, even though not here in the flesh to defend its possible vagaries or idiosyncrasies.

To show it here, therefore, I feel would in a sense defeat its purpose; but I feel free to say of it that in its design I have reversed the usual course of creation and have taken a roman letter (no particular letter) and "gothicized" it, at the same time attempting to retain every feature of interest and legibility of its forbears. It has color, movement and, for many uses, distinction, if one can judge from the large drawings. *Spot* magazine for December, 1942, showed two letters, G and g, which are reproduced herein and which must suffice for present exhibition.

In the summer of 1942, in Los Angeles, I was interviewed by a reporter of the *Los Angeles Times*.

I spoke of this projected face, but the reporter in his account wholly failed (inadvertently, no doubt) to include my statement that the type was to appear *only after my demise*, and I was horrified to find in newspaper notices by the Associated Press that I was working *"on my last type."* I have had dozens of protests from unknown admirers regarding this erroneous publicity; but such publicity, once it gets into print, is impossible to stop.

The type pleases me; it will please some readers; it may be execrated by others; I wish that I might know how it will be received—and maybe I shall!

ABCDEFGHIJKLMNOPQRSTUV
WXYZ .,"´:;!?fiflffffiffl &$1234567890
abcdefghijklmnopqrstuvwxyz

(This full alphabet has been added in this second edition.)
Lanston Monotype issued this face in 1953.

SPENCER OLD STYLE and ITALIC
[Designs No. 112 and No. 113]

During a conversation with a representative of one of the largest book-printing plants in the United States, this gentleman said he would like an exclusive type for certain particular items of its work. I thereupon began the creation of a new book face in roman and italic. I drew some fifty-odd characters to crystallize the design and fix (as far as mere drawings can do so) a comprehensive showing of my ideas. I showed these drawings to the representative referred to. He was delighted with the proposed new letter and it looked as though I would have work ahead for months, when suddenly, bang! Owing to war restrictions, labor troubles, etc., the whole project blew right up in my face, leaving me with some perfectly good sketches on hand. Drawings for type, unless they actually are made into type, are about as useful as a third leg, so I hoped to cut one size to show that there was life in the old boy yet.

Some months later it flashed across my mind that shortly after the fire I had promised to make a type for Syracuse University, a promise which never had been kept, because of inadequate equipment, war restrictions, my ill health, and, I fear, my own procrastination—since no definite deadline had been set. The delay in getting at the promised design was unintentional, as I particularly wished to do the work. The University had been the first educational institution to recognize my work in type design, and in 1939 it had honored me with an L.H.D. (Doctor of Humane Letters); its School of Journalism gave

230

my name to its typographic laboratory; and in 1936 it had bestowed on me its first Medal of Honor, and placed my name on its faculty roster.

Therefore when the commission to do a new type for the printing plant fell through, and I found myself with several sheets of drawings on hand but with no definite destination for them, my long-delayed promise to the University was recalled. An inspection of these sketches convinced me that with a few revisions they might prove a nucleus for the promised Syracuse type. Later I decided (with his permission) to name the face "Spencer Old Style," to honor, in the only way open to me, M. Lyle Spencer, Dean of the Syracuse School of Journalism, in recognition of his many kindnesses to me.

phasg

MISCELLANEOUS WORK

IN THE foregoing story of my type designs I have
intentionally omitted any reference to certain type
characters designed or drawn by others, for which I
engraved the matrices. But I cannot here refrain
from speaking of one such commission of which I
really am proud. In his recently published *Paragraphs on Printing* Bruce Rogers speaks of "a series
of minute diagrams"* (page 162) for which he
allowed me to cut matrices for him. The matrices
were to be used to cast types to accompany Stanley
Morison's text of his monograph for the Grolier
Club on *Luca de Pacioli*, after Rogers' layout. He
does not tell you in *Paragraphs* that he wished an
additional character engraved to accompany the
"minute diagrams" but which he feared was beyond
my technical ability to engrave—that is, he wished
an 18-point type divided into 100 squares. To make
a work pattern for this type really was a difficult
task, but after several attempts I succeeded, and the
type cast from my matrix appears with the others,
all printed on dampened rough handmade paper,
and each of the 100 squares of this special character
is clear and distinct, although they are each less than
.002 inches square. I wish I had space to describe my
solution of the pattern problem involved, which,
after many ineffectual attempts, was simple enough.

*These "minute diagrams" he was intending to repro-
duce by zinc etching which I was sure would not print clean
and sharp, owing to their small size, so I suggested cutting
matrices if he would make drawings for them.

Since the foregoing was written, I recall that back in 1931 I did a little work for my friend Robert Foster, the designer, which properly does not come into this record, as I was merely the instrument by which his work was given type form. He had produced an alphabet which he named "Foster Abstract," too radical in design for any foundry or composing-machine company to include in its list, and while for me it violated every canon of type design, I was yet willing to put his drawings into matrices and cast characters for him—since, after all, the type itself, regardless of my opinion, would show its merits or its lack of them.

HEBREW
[Design No. 114]

ENTERING my eightieth year, it seemed improbable that I should attempt many new projects, or to do more than complete plans already in progress. I did hope, however, to receive a commission, then under consideration, for a new Hebrew type. A Hebrew, to round out my long list of romans, italics, gothics, Greek, etc., would prove an interesting addition.

In April, 1944, I received the commission to make the face. It really doesn't belong in this list of types,

as I am not expected to design the characters, but rather to cut a face based on an old manuscript and give it a typographic quality. Nevertheless the amount of work I shall have to put into it entitles it to at least a mention.

A representative of the Hebrew University of Jerusalem who approached me regarding the new Hebrew face, takes the ground that a Hebrew designer—who I suggested might be of help—would probably find himself so hidebound by his traditions that he might not get into his work the desired quality of freedom that I would. My preliminary study of the Hebrew characters shows me that there is an opportunity to get a new expression in them, just as in the roman. When my drawings were ready for delivery I made several suggestions which I thought would help the design. The New York representative did not care to assume the responsibility for their acceptance, and sent the drawings to Palestine for approval. Since then I've had no word of them.

SCRIPPS COLLEGE ITALIC
[Design No. 115]

In the same mail which brought confirmation of the commission for a Hebrew face, there was also an order to go ahead with the designing of an italic type to accompany the roman (Design No. 110) which I had made in 1941 for the Hartley Alexander Burr Press of Scripps College. The matter of an italic had been under discussion for some weeks and the order to do it was very gratifying. Of course, since it was to accompany a roman already in use, certain features of design were more or less automatically settled; nevertheless an italic which I hoped would present an element of distinction and variety was a problem that gave me pause. Confronted with the fact that designers have worked for practically five hundred years attempting to solve that very same problem, I could not but wonder whether I could produce a design not too reminiscent of other italics, and not commonplace or bizarre, in the attempt to attain something pleasing both to the Press and myself.

When I began the actual drawings from which to cut the matrices, it was, I am free to admit, a moment of trepidation—the start of my hundred-twentieth design. As I have said, some features were "automatically settled": the item of weight, serifs, the height of capitals and lower-case; but the matter of design itself was an item of real concern. I am not sure that I have anywhere in this account of my types told specifically of my methods of working out a design, but one point I may make clear here that it has never been my practice to make preliminary sketches. Maybe I should; but be that as it may, the sketches I do make are usually simply to develop or decide such details as shape of serifs, the form of counters in lower-case a, d, p, and, in the case of an italic, the inclination of the letters and movement of the curved elements. These sketches frequently are drawn to no particular scale and are just as likely to be on the back of a used envelope or a scrap of letter paper, since after all they are merely to set the gray cells to work, and probably will be so modified later when incorporated in the working drawings as to be practically unrecognizable.

In the case of this particular italic, I decided to make simplicity of detail and form the chief desiderata, and rely on subtleness of handling and greater exuberance in the swash letters, rather than on radical departures in the separate characters, for the distinction I wanted for the face. The specimen given must furnish the answer to whether I have succeeded or not.

A B C C E F G H I L N O

P Q R S T U a b c d e f g

h i j l m n o p r s t u y ? , ;

MARLBOROUGH TEXT
[Design No. 122]

LAST fall (1944) I designed a certificate for use of
the International Printing Ink Company. Setting it
in Forum type, I was struck by the monotonous
appearance of my layout, but decided that if the
main line in it could present more color it might
give the whole certificate the accent it needed. I
thereupon began the designing of the words "Certificate of Honor" in a new black letter and made
patterns and cut the matrices for these characters,
which I had cast for me in Chicago. As I worked it
occurred to me that by adding the caps T and D and
the lower-case y, p, g, s, I could form the words
"Type Design," which I have used on the title page
of this chronicle. Several friends have suggested that
I should complete the font but I doubt that I shall
go further with it. My sponsors suggest that this
memo regarding the design should have place in this
account of my type work.

☙ Certificate of
Honor Dgpsy

In 1936 I was honored by a request of the Typophiles to contribute something to its volume in preparation on Ampersands. I had been making ampersands for my types for years without giving much thought to their origin, except that for the greater number of them I endeavored to convey the idea of "et" in each. Beyond that point they hadn't particularly interested me, until one day when my friend Howard Coggeshall, the printer of Utica, asked me what I was doing and I said "I was drawing some ampersands." After about half-an-hour's cogitation he came back with "What the H— is an ampersand"—and I told him. When he had gone I said to myself that if a printer like Howard didn't know what an ampersand was, there must be many writers, typographers, advertisers, etc., who don't know either. So I looked in the dictionary and encyclopedia and found, except for a few lines in each that the matter was almost a secret, so I began looking into it. Of course all this is beside the purposes of the present volume, but as my research led to the drawing and engraving of *sixty-five* ampersands to illustrate my contribution to the Typophile book, I feel that a mention and showing of a few of them here may not be out of place, since they are a part of my type-founding output.

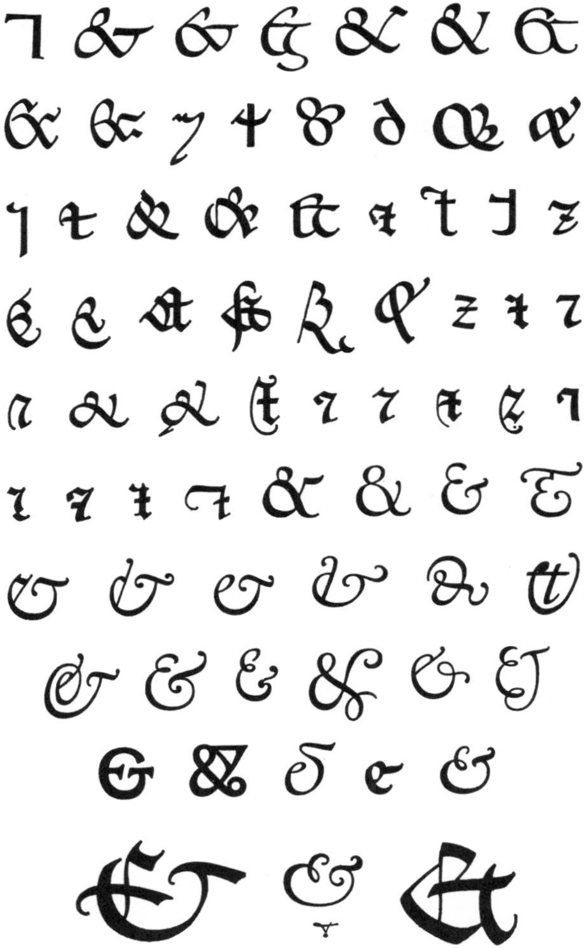

Every now and then when a spot of decoration seemed required in a bit of printing I had in hand, or where sometimes it occurred to me to include a floret or fleuron in a type I was working on, I would engrave it. The idea came to me that since I found such items useful, why not design several as part of my stock in trade? My memory isn't quite clear as to the time I first put up a collection of them for sale, but I find that a specimen of my types prepared for the Continental Typefounders Association, which distributed my types to printers, contained a complete showing of six separate assortments of "Fleurons" made up of some thirty-five different characters, several cut in two or three sizes, including a "pointing hand" mentioned in Chap Book No. VII, but not included among its illustrations. The Continental specimen is dated 1934 so a number must have been made a year or so earlier. They are not really "types," but they are engraved and cast just like type, so I include a showing of them here.

241

BY WAY OF EPILOGUE

A READING of the preceding text indicates that certain after-thoughts, which did not seem to fit into the text itself, demand a place in these annals, so I include them here by way of epilogue.

After reviewing the work to which, for practically a half-century, I have devoted my thought, I should like to interpolate some personal criticisms of that work; for I feel that some of my designs appear a bit less spontaneous in handling than I intended them to be at the time of their making—almost as though certain features in the designs had been "thought" into place—the very thing I have so long and so consistently inveighed against.

In my *Alphabet*, published first in 1918 and revised and enlarged in 1942,* I said: "To attempt consciously to give a specific character or beauty to a letter is too frequently also to exhibit the intellectual processes by which these qualities are sought; its character seems to have been 'thought in,' and does not appear to be the outcome of a subtle and indefinable taste that makes it delightful and, as well, seemingly the obvious and inevitable thing." This dictum reads well, but will it stand a careful analysis? After all, *how* is one to create new expressions except by taking thought? What the artist thinks will show inevitably in the designs he produces.

A letter is beautiful or it isn't; a type is legible or it isn't, and no excellence of technique will insure

*Published by the University of California Press and printed in the types (Nos. 106 and 107 of this chronicle) designed for the Press.

beauty or legibility, or lack of it necessarily result in mediocrity. If the letter is "beautiful" and "legible," what does it matter if those qualities seem to be "thought" into it? The fact that beauty or legibility obviously was sought, doesn't make the type less beautiful or less legible—or does it?

Maybe I don't know just what "spontaneity" in design means. It has been said of my work that my "curves are too sweet" and the statement annoys me, because I don't grasp completely just what the implication is. If they are "sweet," it is because that's the way I work naturally. Giotto, it is said, could draw with a single sweep of his brush as true a circle as another might with a compass or bowpen; da Vinci's work was executed with an incomparable exactness. These men were geniuses, they produced things easily and naturally and got results which ordinarily would be produced by others only with care and thought. Should they deliberately have made their work less perfect to please others less facile than they? Not having the facility of Giotto or Leonardo, it has taken me forty-eight years to acquire a technique of handling by practice and study which will enable me to express my ideas in a manner that will exhibit a degree of order, dignity and beauty, and I hope, at times, a sublimity in design—if that is not too grand a word to apply to a minor art.

I have spoken only incidentally here and there of the actual processes of translating a drawing into the final metal type for which it was conceived. Now a drawing is but one step toward a printing type—an important step, of course, but I feel that here I might also set down more than just the reasons and inspirations for its making and describe briefly the process of its becoming a matrix from which the type itself will be cast.

In my *Typologia*, written for the University of California Press (and published as its contribution to the five-hundredth anniversary of the birth of typography), I have spoken pretty fully of such matters as "What Type Is," "The Design of Types," "The Designer's Problem," "Details of Construction," "Making the Patterns," etc., but as that book may not have come to the eyes of the reader of this one, I have asked the Press for permission to include herein some extracts from my chapter on "Matrix Engraving." With this permission kindly granted, I also repeat something of the philosophy developed through the years regarding type design.

I have said many times that "my craft is a simple one." It is simple because I think simply; my work presents the simplicity that takes account of the essentials but with no intentional neglect for beauty or dignity that makes simple forms pleasing. The boy six or seven years old forms the letters CAT, and they probably present the quintessence of simplicity *as to form*, but they present a simplicity that more likely is mere crudity of outline. I flatter myself that my own letters CAT might be just as simple in form as his, but mine would probably show also the results of a study of the fundamental and traditional aspects of the letters, a sense of proportion, and a beauty possibly due to an innate mechanical sense and a deftness of handling on my part not likely within the boy's capacity.

But there is something still required in addition to the "innate mechanical sense" mentioned when one attempts a design for a simple, legible, dignified, and beautiful type. The designer may be apt, but that fact, of itself, will not prevent anachronisms; he must know also the history and development of letters, the types too, from Gutenberg's time to the present, the designs that have been produced by the masters, and he must be able to perceive and seize upon in their work the things he needs in his own work—the quirks and turns that have caught his attention and fired his imagination, not indeed to copy or to imitate them but, instead, to fuse them in the fire of his own thought into new type creations.

As Stanley Morison, the eminent English writer on typographic matters once wrote, "A good designer knows that for a new type to be successful, it has to be so good that only very few readers recognize its novelty. If the readers do not notice the consummate reticence and rare discipline of a newly designed type it probably is a good letter."

To draw a line by mere mechanical deftness is one thing; to draw a line of delicacy and refinement, subtle and expressive, instinct with life and vigor and variety, is something else and can be done only by one with a due regard and feeling for those qualities.

Fournier says that "matrices are the fruit and product of the punches." In my own work, matrices are the fruit of my original drawings which I transcribe into intaglio metal patterns, from which, in an engraving machine, I cut the matrices in which the types themselves are cast. Fournier engraved steel punches laboriously by hand; I cut large master patterns by hand and from these I engrave *mechanically* the reduced metal patterns from which the matrix itself is engraved.

The late Rudolf Koch, whom I should have liked to know personally, wrote that "the engraving machine is seeking to displace craftsmanship and we must bring pressure to bear in opposition." I am willing to agree with his statement when and if the engraving machine is used simply as a means for mass production of any work; it cannot in the nature of things convey the vitality and personality which would be given by the hand of the designer himself. The important point is to recognize where handwork ends and machine work begins, and see that the facility of the machine is not permitted to usurp or displace any of the functions of creation and representation. To me the appearance of the finished work is of more importance than the method of its translation into the vehicle of thought, since its legibility or beauty is a matter of the eye and not of the means of its production. Craftsmanship is not art; it is the artistic expression of one's self in work destined rather for utilitarian purposes than for esthetic exhibition—it is, nevertheless, art's handmaiden.

I do not believe that the intelligent use of a machine or of machine tools makes a thing bad—it is the evil use of them. When used merely as a tool the machine minimizes labor which, while necessary, is in itself painful and monotonous. The most complicated device is justifiable if it aids in the exact reproduction of the original design, but not if it lessens the manhood of the user or helps to make machines of our souls.

I would like here to interpolate a few words regarding the specimen types accompanying my stories of the various designs. Obviously a mere showing which can at best include two or three characters only of the alphabets displayed, does not constitute a real exhibition of the design itself. It must be evident to any reader that the designer of over a hundred type faces, when he has made the letter "O" (either capital or lower case) for one design, say one of normal width or height or weight, for another one wider or narrower, fatter or leaner (excluding minor subtleties of handling), he has about exhausted the possibilities of differences (unless he resorts to some freakish or bizarre shape) and he must therefore necessarily include in some of his designs, "O's" practically identical in form. This is true of lower case "l's", "s's", "v's", "c's", etc.

How then, does one evaluate an original type design? When we speak of design, we commonly mean invention, and we cannot reasonably expect any striking departures in the forms of individual letters, since the essential letter forms are fixed. But we may give to one face of type a quality of distinction, or of novelty which will differ in a page of text from the qualities presented by another face of the same general character similarly employed. It is this difference in expression exhibited by the types in mass which is not at once evident by the showing of individual letters, and it is this different expression which I call design.

I imagine that if an 18-pt. Caslon lower case "a"

were shown along side a Garamond a, a Baskerville a, a Cloister a, a Kennerley a, a Deepdene a, an Italian O. S. a (in which this book is set), or any other a's of the same character and point size, not one printer in a hundred could name them off-hand correctly. But a block of the same text matter set in the types from which the "a's" were taken would be recognized immediately by the different expression given.

Yet this does not mean that every letter must present some actual and demonstrable difference in outline and appearance, or even that it need exhibit a different set of proportional measurements when compared with other existing forms of the same letter. If my contentions are correct, design then, is not so much a matter which concerns the shapes we give to the individual characters which make up the new font as it is a matter that concerns the printed appearance of the page as a whole. (Here the reader may be allowed a grain of salt because in spite of what I've said, I do attempt to get into individual letters something of myself—personality, for want of a better term.)

Few readers are competent to decide whether a type face advertised as "new" is really new, or is merely a revival of an older type that probably was entirely suitable to earlier conditions; or even whether it is the product of a designer with facility of draughtsmanship but without knowledge of the development or traditions of the craft he practises.

I have long since ceased to care for (no, that isn't quite true: I do care—but I have ceased to expect) any great appreciation of the results realized after over forty years of study and practice in type design; and now, since I seem to have reached a definite and recognized standing in the field, I endeavor still to maintain a complete indifference to public opinion; the versatility and imagination displayed in my work must be my very own, not tempered by the suggestions of others, in the hope that, at times, it may even reach the heights of sublimity.

"In describing my method of engraving matrices I wish it clearly understood that I am describing a method I *devised for my own use.* I realize fully that a type foundry or a composing-machine company operating on a large scale would find my method not entirely practicable. My method differs (from theirs) more in the simplicity of its materials than in its actual operation, and I am not intending to imply that it is better than that employed elsewhere; I maintain simply that I have found it sufficiently accurate, direct, and expeditious for my own requirements." And I wish also to emphasize my position regarding my work in matrix engraving: "Ambrose-Firmin Didot said of Fournier's punch cutting that 'it was far from perfect in finish,' and I have no doubt that the same criticism might also be made of my own matrix engraving. I am more interested in the printed appearance of my designs *as types* than I am in the details of their manufacture, and I am not setting myself up as a matrix cutter or type founder in competition with workmen who have followed for years the various mechanical details of type founding. I care nothing for the criticism of my work (the mechanical side of it) since *I cut matrices only to insure that my types will be artistic*

249

products completed in the spirit in which they are designed, instead of mere interpretations of my drawings by another hand. As probably no one will attempt to use this account of my work as a manual of matrix-cutting technique, I will not therefore do more than describe the essentials of it.

"When the original drawings have been made . . . the next step is the making of a pattern that will retain the subtleties and disciplined freedom of them." The pattern which I found to answer my purpose I have described more or less completely in my account of Design No. 54, so I will not amplify those comments here, except to say that when I began my type-founding work I used a pattern nine inches high instead of seven and one-half inches as I now do.* This large paper pattern I employ in turn to engrave an intaglio work pattern in a plate of type metal about one-tenth of an inch thick; this plate I cast in a stereotyping box. This metal pattern is placed on the table of an upright engraving machine and locked in place. The matrix-engraving machine I found to be entirely satisfactory for my work was not primarily made for such work, but with a few alterations which the manufacturer kindly made for me . . . it performed my work accurately; and—what was quite important—the machine, with alterations, did not cost more than I could afford.

"It contains an upright pantograph; at the lower end it carries a tracer which is ball-shaped, and at

*For Design No. 100 I tried using a six inch pattern, but did not find it as satsifactory as my seven and one-half inch ones.

250

the upper end a movable table on which a matrix blank is fastened. As the tracer moves around within the walls of the pattern letter, the matrix block also moves in similar manner but in reduced degree (i.e., to the size of the type desired). Since the arm carrying the tracer moves in various directions to and from an absolute perpendicular, the ball-shaped tracer, being of constant diameter, maintains its center always at the same distance from the pattern wall, and relatively the center of the cutter is at the same distance proportionately. The cutting tool is in the exact ratio to the tracer as the type desired is to the pattern letter. The table carrying the matrix blank to be engraved 'rests on ball bearings and is sensitive to the slightest movement of the tracing point. Directly above the matrix blank is a machine head which carries a small cutting tool (which I grind and sharpen to a form I devised) at the lower end of a spindle which revolves at high speed . . . and bores its way into the matrix blank as the blank follows the movement of the tracer to a depth controlled by a micrometer adjustment' set for the exact depth desired. To maintain the exact width of the cutting tool selected requires constant examination of the cutting point under a high-powered microscope equipped with a micrometer eyepiece calibrated in thousandths of an inch."

I WOULD like to end this Epilogue with a bit of personal information, probably unimportant in itself, but possibly of bibliographical interest in years to come: that up to 1925 I had never attempted to cut a matrix, since that sort of work had been so admirably done for me by my friend Robert Wiebking of Chicago. His death in 1927 left me with no one to turn to for such work.

I have told, in my story of Design No. 56, of my commission to make a type for the *Woman's Home Companion*. To carry out the commission I attempted with no previous type-founding experience, or "tutelage" under any master, to learn every detail of type founding—making patterns, grinding cutting tools, engraving matrices—*after* I had passed my sixtieth birthday.

A large majority of the designs since No. 56 have, of course, been engraved in matrix form by myself, using methods I have described elsewhere. By using my machines as instruments of my own hand, I have been enabled in these designs to achieve the exact effects I have desired—an effective answer to those critics who have maintained that the machine is an obstructive intervention between the artist and the finished type.

A BIBLIOGRAPHY OF THE PUBLISHED
WRITINGS OF FREDERIC W. GOUDY

By George L. McKay

The following record deals with Goudy as author and editor exclusively. The late Melbert B. Cary's admirable and beautifully printed *Bibliography of the Village Press*, 1938, is concerned with FWG as printer and type designer. Since Goudy printed some of his own writings, the two bibliographies overlap to that extent. The present list does not record certain items that might be regarded as within its scope: entries have not been included for announcements or prospectuses of books printed at the Village Press or of types designed by Goudy, invitations, notices and other such ephemera. Although Goudy wrote many of these items, they have not been regarded as his WRITINGS for purposes of this bibliography. Much of this fugitive material, if printed by the maestro, has been apprehended in Cary's work—to which the reader is respectfully referred.

PART I

BOOKS AND OTHER SEPARATELY PRINTED ITEMS WRITTEN OR EDITED BY FREDERIC W. GOUDY

1

[American Cat News.] Chicago, cir. 1901.

Mr. Goudy was editor of this short-lived periodical. I have seen no copy of any number, nor is the periodical listed [at least with the above title] in the Union List of Serials, 1943.

2

Typographica. No. 1[-6]. New York, 1911[-1934]. Illus., type specimens. Size of leaf varies.

Edited by Mr. Goudy. Except for the word "Typographica," the title varies. Described in no. 2 as "an occasional pamphlet treating of printing, letter-design, and allied arts." No. 1 was issued September, 1911; no. 2: June, 1912; no. 3: March, 1916; Supplement to no. 3: October, 1916; no. 4: July, 1926; no. 5: summer, 1927; no. 6: fall, 1934.

3

Why / we have chosen / Forest Hills / Gardens / for our Home / [illus.] / Forest Hills Gardens • N • Y • / MCM•XV / [14] leaves. Front., illus. Leaf: 9 x 6 inches.

Colophon: "This booklet . . . has been arranged by Frederic W. Goudy at the suggestion and with the co-operation of Will Phillip Hooper. Decorations and types designed by Mr. Goudy and set by Bertha M. Goudy . . ."

The introduction was written by Mr. Goudy, and also 7 lines bearing his name in the body of the book.

4

Ars Typographica / Volume I Spring 1918 Number I / [-Autumn, 1934 Number 4] / Illus., ports., facsims., ornaments, type specimens. Leaf: 12½ x 8⅛ inches.

Four numbers, edited by Mr. Goudy. No. 1 was issued in the spring, 1918; no. 2: summer, 1918; no. 3: spring, 1920; and no. 4: autumn, 1934. The first three numbers were issued by The Marchbanks Press, and the fourth by the Press of the Woolly Whale. Before no. 4 of Vol. I was issued, Vols. II and III were published under the editorship of Douglas C. McMurtrie.

5

The / Alphabet / Fifteen / Interpretative Designs / Drawn and Arranged with / Explanatory Text and / Illustrations / By / Frederic W. Goudy / [ornament] / New York / Mitchell Kennerley / MCMXVIII / [1] leaf, 44 pp., [29] leaves. Front., alphabets, type specimens. Leaf: 12¾ x 9⅝ inches.

Type set by Bertha M. Goudy; printed by William

Edwin Rudge; plates made by the Walker Engraving Co. Published in London in 1922 by John Lane.

6

The / City of Crafts / A Phantasy / Being some Account / of a Journey to the Court of the / Printers' Guild / Told by / A member of the American Institute / of Graphic Arts of what he saw and / heard there, and the printers he talked / with; illustrated by pictures with a lan- / tern at a meeting of the Institute on the / evening of Wednesday, February 15, 1922 / [ornament] / New York / American Institute of Graphic Arts / 1922 [10] leaves. Front. (port.), head- and tail-pieces, initial letter. Leaf: 9½ x 6 inches.

Decorations by George Illian. Printed by William Edwin Rudge. Issued also without decorations, in paper wrappers, for distribution on the night of the meeting, February 15, 1922.

7

Elements of / Lettering / <With XIII Full-page Plates> / By / Frederic W. Goudy / Author of The Alphabet. Editor, Ars Typographica / Text composed by Bertha M. Goudy in types / designed by the Author / [device] / New York: Mitchell Kennerley / 1922 / [2] leaves, 48, [3] pp. Front., type specimens. Leaf: 12¾ x 9½ inches.

Printed at the Marchbanks Press. Published in London in 1922 by John Lane.

The Anderson Galleries, New York / [device of The Village Press] / This Keepsake / is the first impression made in America on / the hand-press formerly owned by William / Morris, now the property of Frederic and Bertha Goudy, and is printed by them for / visitors at an Exhibiion of that press and / of their work at The Village Press. / March M,cm,xxiv / Broadside, 11¾ x 8½ inches. Ornamental border.

9

The Type Speaks / Broadside, 8½ x 11 inches.
"Designed, engraved and composed" by Mr. Goudy. Only a few proofs pulled, December 30, 1931; never distributed. Reprinted several times both in broadside and pamphlet form, by Mr. Goudy and others. The first issue to be distributed was apparently the broadside printed in connection with the Retrospective Exhibition of The Village Press, organized by the American Institute of Graphic Arts, and held at the Museum of Science and Industry, New York City, October 23-November 19, 1933. Cf. M. B. Cary, Jr., A Bibliography of The Village Press.

The Story of the / Village Type / by its designer / Frederic W. Goudy / [monogram] / New York / The Press of the Woolly Whale / 1933 / [3] leaves, 13, [1] pp., [7] leaves. Leaf: 9 x 6⅛ inches.
Printed in Village No. 2 and Goudy Antique types, their first appearance in any book.

Design and Beauty / in Printing / by / Frederic W. Goudy / [ornament] / Printed by the / Press of the Woolly Whale / on his 69th Birthday / March 8, 1934 / [2] leaves, 18 pp., [1] leaf. Leaf: 5⅞ x 4½ inches.

Printed in 14-point revised Goudy Village No. 2 type, used for the first time in this book. Reprinted, somewhat abridged, with the title: Beauty & Design in Printing / By Frederic W. Goudy, in The Pacific Printer and Publisher, Vol. LVII, No. 6, San Francisco, June, 1937, p. 22. This was an address given by Mr. Goudy at Columbia University a few months before his 69th birthday.

12

The / Capitals / from the / Trajan Column / at Rome / By / Frederic W. Goudy / With xxv plates / drawn & engraved [on wood] by the author / [monogram] / New York / Oxford University Press / 1936 / [iii]-xi, [1], 20 pp., [27] leaves. Plate, alphabets, diagr. Leaf: 10 x 6½ inches.

Printed in Village and Trajan types, being the first use of the Village italics.

A Tribute to B•M•G / Broadside, 9½ x 6¾ inches. Signed and dated (typographically) at the bottom: F•W•G / Marlboro, June, 1936 / The tribute was re-issued as a 4-page keepsake for participants in the celebration of the thirty-fifth anniversary of the Village Press at Deepdene, Saturday, July 23, 1938.

Hello Everybody / This Is / Goudy / Speaking /
Now friends, we bring you / that great star of the
radio, / screen and the Graphic Arts / Frederic W.
Goudy, / In Person / New York / The Maveric
Press / 1936 / [4] leaves. Leaf: 6⅞ x 4⅝ inches.

Excerpt from a broadcast conducted by Mr. Lowell
Thomas, with Mr. Goudy's answers to Mr.
Thomas's questions, over the NBC Network, Sta-
tion WJZ, on Monday, September 17, 1934. Edi-
tion of 100 copies printed by Earl H. Emmons in
Goudy Deepdene italic type, being item no. 5 of the
Maveric Press in New York.

15

Types / of the Past • Type Revivals / with a few
Words on Type Design / in General / An Address
at the / New York Press Association Dinner / September 12 • MCMXXXVI / By Frederic W.
Goudy / With a Foreword by Howard Coggeshall /
and a Presentation by M. Lyle Spencer, Dean of /
the School of Journalism / [seal of the University] /
Syracuse, New York / School of Journalism / Syracuse University / 1936 / [14] leaves, including fly-
leaves which contain watermark portrait of Mr.
Goudy. Leaf: 9⅛ x 6¾ inches.

16

Type Revivals / An Exposition / regarding / Inde-
pendent new Designs / By Frederic W. Goudy /
[ornament] / Lexington, Virginia / Journalism
Laboratory Press / Washington and Lee University /
1937 / [3]-18, [1] pp. Leaf: 6½ x 4¼ inches.

17

The Bible / An Address by Frederic W. Goudy on the occasion of / the presentation of the Oxford Lectern Bible / to / The New York School of Printing / on May 18th, 1938 / [ornament] / New York City: / The New York School of Printing / mcmxxxviii / [2] leaves, 8, [1] pp. Leaf: 9¾ x 7 inches.

Edition of 200 copies printed in Mr. Goudy's Friar type.

18

B•M•G / [rule] / Bertha M. Goudy / Recollections / by one / who Knew her Best / [monogram] / Marlboro, N. Y. / The Village Press / MCMXXXIX / [2] leaves, 33 pp. Front., il., ports. Front. and t.p. within ornamented border. Leaf: 10½ x 7 inches. Printed in Bertham type. The memorial is here reprinted in separate form, with an introduction and some additional matter, from Bookmaking / on the / Distaff / Side / [ornament] / Mcmxxxvii / [136] leaves. Leaf: 7½ x 4½ inches. The memorial occupies [12] leaves in this book. Port. of Mrs. Goudy.

19

What Printing Is / By / Frederic W. Goudy / [ornament] / Messinger Paper Company / Chicago / 1940 / [1] leaf, 11 pp. Leaf: 5¾ x 4¾ inches.

Reprinted from Ars Typographica, Vol. I, No. 2, New York, Summer, 1918, pp. 37-40; and from Goudy Gaudeamus / In celebration of the dinner /

given Frederic W. Goudy / on his 74th birthday / March eighth / 1939 / Printed for the Distaff Side/ 1939 /. In the latter book Mr. Goudy's article occupies a 4-leaf section with title: What / Printing Is : [monogram] / Greetings to the Author of / this Monograph, on His / Seventy-fourth Birthday / Frederic W. Goudy / Typographic Laboratory / Syracuse University.

20

Typologia / Studies in Type Design & Type Making / with Comments on the Invention of Typography • The First Types / Legibility and Fine / Printing / [ornament] / Frederic W. Goudy, L.H.D. Litt.D. / ∴ / Berkeley and Los Angeles / University of California Press / 1940 [iii]-xviii, [2], 170, [1] pp. Front., il., ports., facsims., type specimens. Leaf: 10¼ x 6¾ inches.

Printed in California Old Style type, designed for the University of California by Mr. Goudy and used for the first time in this book.

21

The Design / of Types / [ornament] / Frederick [sic] W. Goudy / [cover title.] [8] leaves. Leaf: 8⅜ x 5½ inches.

Address delivered May 10, 1941, to the Second District Conference of the International Association of Printing House Craftsmen held at Gloversville, N. Y., and sponsored by the Adirondack Club. Edition of 300 copies published by the Adirondack Club of Printing House Craftsmen.

22

The / Alphabet / and Elements of Lettering / Revised and Enlarged / with many full-page Plates and other / Illustrations Drawn & Arranged / by the Author / Frederic W. Goudy / L.H.D., Litt.D. / [device] / Berkeley and Los Angeles / University of California Press / 1942 / xv, [1], 101, [1] pp., [28] leaves. Front., facsims., alphabets, type specimens. Leaf: 12⅝ x 9⅜ inches.

Printed in California Old Style type. The University Press, having no italic of this face larger than 14-point, set the Preface in type of that size, and then made zinc etchings to enlarge the size to 18-point, the size used for the text set in roman.

PART II

CONTRIBUTIONS BY
FREDERIC W. GOUDY
TO BOOKS AND PERIODICALS

23

A few Words by way of Pro- / logue: Being an Explanation, / an Advertisement, and an In- / vitation. (In: The Black Art / A Homily By / D. B. Updike / [ornament] / Reprinted by permission, from / The Engraver and Printer for / January 1894, to which is added / a Prologue by Fred. W. Goudy / Cover-page is by Berne Nadall / [ornament] / The Camelot Press / Chicago / [8] leaves. Leaf: 6 x 4½ inches). Mr. Goudy's prologue occupies both sides of the third leaf, and is dated at end: February MDCCC-XCV.

The Homily and prologue were reprinted in: Goudy Gaudeamus / In celebration of the dinner / given Frederic W. Goudy / on his 74th birthday / March eighth / 1939 / Printed for the Distaff Side: 1939 / Partly colored illus., ornaments. Leaf: 6⅛ x 4½ inches. The reprint, done in 10-point Deepdene type by the Press of the Woolly Whale, occupies the last [6] leaves of this book.

24

Notes on Letter Design / By Frederic W. Goudy / (In: The Graphic Arts for Printers and Users of Printing, Vol. I, No. 5, Boston, May, 1911, pp. 361-368. Plate, type specimens.)

25

Quality in Printing* / By Frederic W. Goudy / (In: The Printing Art, Vol. XXVI, No. 4, Cambridge, Mass., December, 1915, pp. 281-285).

26

Typographica / Edited by Frederic W. Goudy / (In: Photographic Art, Vol. 3, No. 2, New York, October, 1917, p. 19).

*Read at the United Typothetæ Convention at Los Angeles, 1915.

Type Designs: Old and New (In: Ars Typographica, Vol. I, No. 1, New York, Spring, 1918, pp. [38]-40).

The author's initials, F. W. G., are printed at the end.

The Editor's Workshop (In: Ars Typographica, Vol. I, No. 1, New York, Spring, 1918, pp. [45]-47).

The Editor's Workshop (In: Ars Typographica, Vol. I, No. 2, New York, Summer, 1918, pp. 41-45).

Hand-Press Printing: A Plea / for a lost Craft / By Frederic W. Goudy / (In: Ars Typographica, Vol. I, No. 3, New York, Spring, 1920, pp. 33-35).

Printing as an Art (In: Ars Typographica, Vol. I, No. 3, New York, Spring, 1920, pp. 39-40).

The author's initials, F. W. G., are printed at the end.

The Editor's Workshop (In: Ars Typographica, Vol. I, No. 3, New York, Spring, 1920, pp. 41-44).

• The Craftsman's Ideal • (In: The American Printer, Craftsmen Number, New York, July 5, 1921, [1] unnumbered p. with blank verso).

The author's initials, F. W. G., are printed at the bottom of the article.

34

The First Types* / By Frederic W. Goudy / (In: Monotype A Journal of Composing-Room Efficiency, Vol. VIII, No. 12, Philadelphia, September, 1921, pp. [3]-6).

35

Initial Letters / their Ethics and Aesthetics / By Fred W. Goudy / (In: Monotype A Journal of Composing-Room Efficiency, Vol. IX, No. 2, Philadelphia, March-April, 1922, pp. [18]-20).

36

A Study in Type Design / By / Frederic W. Goudy / (In: Monotype A Journal of Composing-Room Efficiency, Vol. IX, No. 4, Philadelphia, July-August, 1922, pp. 9-11. Facsim., type specimens).

37

The Worm Turns / Admiration for Work of Old Masters in Type Design no Reason for Supposing Further Advance in the Art / Impossible. Present Generation Should not Rest Content with Idolatrous Worship of Achievements of / the Past. Changing Times and Conditions Create Need for New Designs. / By Frederic W. Goudy / (In: Western Advertising, Vol. VI, No. 1, San Francisco, February, 1924, pp. 40 and 42. Port.).

*"Paraphrased extracts from Mr. Goudy's forthcoming book, 'Typologia.' "

38

Introductory Note (In: American Type Design / in the Twentieth Century / With Specimens of the outstanding / Types produced during this Period / By Douglas C. McMurtrie • With an / Introduction by Frederic W. Goudy / [ornament] / Chicago, Illinois / Robert O. Ballou / 1924 / 64 pp. Facsim., type specimens, head-pieces, initial letters. Leaf: 9 x 5¾ inches.)

The introduction is on pp. 5-10.

On the Design of Types / With special Reference to the Types of / The Architectural Record / By Frederic W. Goudy / (In: The Architectural Record, Vol. 63, No. 5, New York, May, 1928, pp. 441-445. Type specimens).

Art in Type-Design / By Frederic W. Goudy / (In: Monotype A Journal of Composing-Room Efficiency, Goudy Number, Philadelphia, November, 1928, pp. 5-7).

Besides Mr. Goudy's article, this issue is devoted to the presentation of Monotype Goudy faces.

Fine Printing / on Fine Papers. / (In: Old / Stratford / Book Papers / A few Specimen Pages and / an Introductory Note on Fine Printing / By / Frederic W. Goudy / [ornament] / Mittineague Mills / Strathmore Paper Company / Mittineague, Massachusetts / [1929]. [20] leaves. Illus., ornaments, paper specimens. Leaf: 9¼ x 6⅛ inches).

Mr. Goudy's note is on 3 pages following the title leaf. The types used for the cover and title-page were drawn and engraved especially for this book. It was an unrealized wish of Mr. Goudy's to have these designs used for a type face for general distribution.

42

Type Design: Past & Present / A Typographic Homily / By Fred. W. Goudy / (In: Monotype, Vol. XXIII, No. 74, Philadelphia, March, 1930, pp. 3-4).

This issue has a special cover title, beginning: Deepdene . . .

43

To Squeeze or not to Squeeze / By Frederic W. Goudy / (In: Monotype, Vol. XXIII, No. 74, Philadelphia, March, 1930, p. 11).

This issue has a special cover title, beginning: Deepdene . . .

44

Foreword / By Frederic W. Goudy / (In: Fashions / in American Typography / 1780 to 1930 / With brief illustrated Stories of / the Life and Environment of the / American People in seven Periods / and Demonstrations of / E. G. G.'s Fresh Note / American Period Typography / By Edmund G. Gress / Author "The Art and Practice of Typography" / [device] / New York / Harper & Brothers

Publishers / 1931 / xxviii pp., [1] leaf, 201 pp. Front., illus., facsims. Leaf: 9⅛ x 6 inches).

The foreword is on pp. v-vii. Some lines on the title-page and the chapter headings were set in a face especially designed by Mr. Goudy for this book and which was later made into a type for commercial use.

45

A Note on the / Marks of the Early Italian / Printers / (In: The Colophon, Part 5, New York, 1931, [1] leaf near end of issue).

Mr. Goudy's Note was set in a new type, Truesdell, especially cut by him for this item; and the article on the three following leaves: The Devices / of the Early Italian Printers / By Carlo Castellani / was set in Mr. Goudy's Mediaeval type—the first use of this face.

46

On Designing a Type-Face / by Frederic W. Goudy / (In: The Dolphin, a Journal of the Making of Books, No. 1, New York, 1933, pp. 3-23. Facsims.).

47

Printer's Note (In: The / Old and the New / a Friendly Dispute / between Juvenis & Senex / By / Theodore Low De Vinne / with a Note by / Frederic W. Goudy / [ornament] / Marlborough, N. Y. / The Village Press / 1933 / [8] leaves. Leaf: 9¾ x 6¼ inches.

The printer's note is on three pp. following the title-leaf. 300 copies of the pamphlet were printed: 230 with a 4-line colophon, and 70 with a 7-line colophon "for presentation to members of the Twelfth Annual Conference on Printing Education on the occasion of their visit to the Village Press, June 25, 1933."

48

On the Thirtieth Birthday / of the Village Press / (A Paper Read by Frederic W. Goudy at the Opening of the / Village Press Exhibit; Museum of Science and Industry, / New York, October 22, 1933) / (In: News-Letter of The American Institute of Graphic Arts, No. 34, New York, March, 1934, pp. 3 and 4).

49

Type Design / a Homily / I. The Force of Tradition • II. Type, What It Is / III. The Technique of Type Engraving / by Frederic W. Goudy / (In: Ars Typographica, Vol. I, No. 4, New York, Autumn, 1934, pp. [3]-27. Ports.).

50

Evening at Deepdene (In: Ars Typographica, Vol. I, No. 4, New York, Autumn, 1934, p. [35]).
The following is printed at the end: < F. W. G., Nov. 1923 >

51

The Editor's Workshop (In: Ars Typographica, Vol. I, No. 4, New York, Autumn, 1934, pp. [47]-50).

52

Retrospectus / [ornament] / An Open Letter / From a Designer of Types to the Greatest / Arranger of Them / (In: . . . / Barnacles from many Bottoms / Scraped and Gathered for / B R / . . . / by The Typophiles / 1935 / [111] leaves. Front. (port.), illus., ornaments. Leaf: 8¾ x 6 inches.

Mr. Goudy's letter occupies four leaves near the front of the book; his pen-and-ink signature is entered at the end of the letter.

53

F. W. G. on typography today / An informal interview with the veteran American type designer / (In: P M An intimate Journal for Production Managers, Art Directors and their Associates, Vol. I, No. 8, New York, April, 1935, pp. 4-6).

54

Ands / & Ampersands / from the First Century B.C. / to the Twentieth A.D. / By / a Type Designer / [monogram] / New York / The Typophiles / 1936 / (In: Diggings / from many ampersandhogs / The Typophiles / [illus.] / Christmas 1936 / Partly colored illus., ornaments, type specimens. Leaf: 5⅛ x 3¾ inches).

Mr. Goudy's monograph has a separate title-page and is separately paged: 52, [2] pp. It was composed and printed (in Deepdene type) by Howard Coggeshall in Utica, N. Y. The monograph was reprinted as a separate pamphlet.

55

The Address of Acceptance / By Frederic • W • Goudy / (In: Ulster-Irish Society / Incorporated / Founded 1927 / Year Book 1937 / [cover title]. 48 pp., [4] leaves. Illus., ports. Leaf: 9¼ x 6 inches).

The address, occupying pp. 15-24, was delivered at the annual banquet of the Ulster-Irish Society of New York held on March 19, 1937, at the Hotel Commodore, New York City, in accepting a medal presented to him "for notable service to the nation" by the Society.

56

Introduction. (In: Goudy / Master of Letters / By / Vrest Orton / [ornament] / With an Introduction by / Frederic W. Goudy / [ornament] / The Black Cat Press / Chicago 1939. / [5]-101, [1] pp., [2] leaves. Front., illus., facsims., ports. Leaf: 8½ x 5½ Inches).

The Introduction occupies pp. 19-23.

Introduction. (In: The Story of / Frederic W. Goudy / Written by Peter Beilenson and printed / with a pictorial supplement / for The Distaff Side / 1939. / 58 pp., [2] leaves. Plates, ports. Leaf: 9⅜ x 6⅜ inches).

The Introduction occupies pp. [5-6].

The Craft / of the Printer / by Frederic W. Goudy / (In: Bibliography / of the Grabhorn Press / • 1915 •

1940 • / By Elinor Raas Heller & / David Magee /
[foregoing five lines within border] / San Francisco •
California • MCMXL / xiv, [6], 193, [2] pp.
Plates, facsims. Leaf: 14 x 10 inches).

Mr. Goudy's introduction is on pp. ix-xiv, plus [1] p;

59

The Ethics and Aesthetics of Type / and Typog-
raphy / An address delivered at Carnegie Institute
of / Technology, Pittsburgh, February 12, 1938 / by
Frederic W. Goudy. / (In: Behind the Type / The
Life Story of Frederic W. Goudy / by Bernard Lewis
/ Issued by the Department of / Printing • Carnegie
Institute / of Technology • Pittsburgh / Nineteen
Forty-one. / [6] leaves, 113, [1] pp. Front., illus.,
Ports. Leaf: 9¼ x 6¼ inches).

The address occupies pp. 103-113.

A NOTE ON THIS BOOK
AND ITS AUTHOR

JUST ten years ago the Typophiles published their first book. *Spinach From Many Gardens* we called it, as we hurriedly put it together to salute Fred Goudy on his seventieth birthday.

This book has not been produced that way. Its writing, in fact, has occupied Mr. Goudy for more than two years—not steadily, but through the weeks and months. In putting down recollections of his many type faces, fresh facts were recalled and the text amplified and edited again and again.

In setting specimens of Goudy type faces to illustrate the text, more than a dozen loyal friends in cities far and near have been of material assistance. Our grateful indebtedness to these contributors, and to other generous Typophiles who have been of invaluable help in production, is detailed on following pages.

We planned and worked to have this book ready for Mr. Goudy's eightieth birthday, March 8, 1945. Conditions beyond our control prevented, unfortunately, and it was not possible to present a copy to each of the two hundred guests at a birthday dinner in his honor at the Ambassador Hotel in New York.

Earnest Elmo Calkins, the distinguished author and advertising agent, put into words, in a letter read that evening, a feeling about F.W.G. that every Typophile would endorse: "The first time I saw Goudy," he recalled, "he was pulling proofs on an old-fashioned lever press as part of some exhibition at the National Arts Club.

"Goudy in his brown linen apron, peering at a proof through his spectacles, looked like an engraving of a historic moment in the art of printing, and I realized that it was a historic moment, and Goudy was just what he seemed to be, a medieval craftsman. He brings to his work the fine unselfish spirit of an earlier age when men were more concerned with the quality of their work than with financial rewards. He was one of a long line of creative workers who have permanently bettered the alphabet—such men as Tory, Dürer, Garamond, Caslon, Morris.

"But while Goudy is medieval in a certain old-fashioned indifference to modern standards of success, his faces are as modern as a patent quoin. He is an old-style face upon a modern body. He has given us many new and beautiful types and has shown us some of the ways they can be used to make beautiful books, but the real measure of his achievement is the extent to which his types are adapted to present-day needs. There is nothing academic about him. He understands that printing is a means to an end. He will be better known to future generations than he is to us. He will be looked back upon as one of the great influences in the history of typography. He is our old master."

And so this book, an ambitious venture for amateurs—yet one, we hope, that may at least separate legend from fact and help keep the record straight in the years ahead.

Mr. Goudy remarks occasionally upon the honors that have come "in the Autumn of my life." Yet it was in 1904, at the Louisiana Purchase Exposition in St. Louis, that his first bronze medal award came for book printing. In 1920 he received the gold medal of the American Institute of Graphic Arts (he is an ex-president of the A.I.G.A. as well as an honorary life member). Two years later he was awarded the craftsmanship gold medal of the American Institute of Architects "for distinguished achievement in the art of typography"; in 1927 he received the Michael Friedsam gold medal at the Architectural League "for service in the cause of industrial art"; and in 1937, the Hon. Frances Perkins, then Secretary of Labor, presented the annual medal of the Ulster-Irish Society of New York "for creations in typographic design that will live forever."

He has been awarded honorary degrees by three institutions of higher education: Doctor of Humane Letters, Syracuse University, in 1939; Doctor of Literature, Mills College, in 1940; Doctor of Laws, University of California, in 1942. The citation that accompanied the latter proudly records the University of California's satisfaction with its private type: "A spiritual descendant of Aldus, Bodoni and Caslon and a master of matrix making who has added to the distinction of the publications of the University by the simplicity and beauty of the type he has designed for them. A triumphant individualist in a world of technology, who has come to lead all his fellows in what is truly the art of letters."

Among his other awards are the medal of honor of the School of Journalism, Syracuse University, in 1936; the Harry J. Friedman gold memorial medal, 1942, "for distinguished service in the cause of graphic arts education," and the medal award of the University of Missouri "for distinguished service to Journalism," 1944. He is an honorary member of the Society of Printers, Boston, and the Montreal, New York and San Francisco Clubs of Printing House Craftsmen.

For the Typophiles it is my privilege to acknowledge here our gratitude to the author, and to many generous friends who have helped so much in the building of this book: Peter Beilenson has been responsible for its design and for seeing it through the press at his Walpole Printing Office, Mount Vernon, New York. A. Colish, New York, has handled the text composition, and the Photogravure and Color Company, New York, has produced the frontispiece for each volume. The collotype reproductions of the Goudy types not possible to include as specimens in letterpress have been produced under the care of E. Harold Hugo at the Meriden Gravure Company. George L. McKay, curator of the Grolier Club, New York, has compiled the bibliography of Mr. Goudy's writings. The binding has been produced by the J. F. Tapley Company, Long Island City, New York, under the supervision of Robert H. Wessmann. The cloth for the binding has been supplied by Albert Clayburgh Jr. of Albert D. Smith & Co., New York.

For the specimen settings of type faces included with the accounts of each type, we are chiefly indebted to: John Archer, Amos Bethke, Howard Coggeshall, E. M. Diamant, Dorothy M. Drake, Samuel T. Farquhar, Jane Grabhorn, Sol Hess, G.

John Morean, Gerry Powell, Frank Powers, C. E. Ruckstuhl, Edna and Arthur W. Rushmore, Albert Schiller, and David Silve. Cooperating organizations and institutions include: Advertising Agencies Service Company, Diamant Typographic Service, and Typographic Service Company, New York; American Type Founders Sales Corporation, Elizabeth, N. J.; the Golden Hind Press, Madison, N. J.; Howard Coggeshall, and Walters Electrotype Company, Utica, N. Y.; the Colt Press, San Francisco; Crowell-Collier Publishing Company, Springfield, Ohio; Lanston Monotype Machine Company, Philadelphia, Penna.; Scripps College, Claremont, California, and the University of California Press, Berkeley, California.

PAUL A. BENNETT

New York, April, 1945.

A LIST OF GOUDY TYPES
By date; for alphabetical list, see Page 282

281

INDEX OF THE TYPES

(Mr. Goudy's design number is indicated by the
italic numerals directly after typeface name)

284

THE CHANGES MADE FROM
THE TYPOPHILES EDITION
(*See the publisher's note, Page* 3)

Vol. I (through Page 142) and Vol. II (starting with Page 143) have been combined, eliminating a second-volume frontispiece in photogravure of "Goudy—Honorary Academician" in academic robes, and half-titles and title page repeated from volume one, all unnumbered. The first-volume frontispiece was "Goudy—Craftsman," showing him at his microscope. Because these photogravures could not be reproduced well, the present volume uses a different photograph of Goudy at his pantograph, as the one frontispiece, reproduced offset.

In the original, the Typophiles logotype and the words "Type Design" on the title page were printed in russet.

Rearrangement of materials moved the Prologue from Pages 7-8 to 13-14, the List of Goudy Types from 9-12 to 278-281, Goudy's Introduction from 15-33 to 18-36, the Index of the Types from 253-256 to 282-285, and the Bibliography from 259-277 to 254-272. The numbering of the main body of the book (the annotated listing of the type designs, from Page 37 to 241) and the Epilogue, Pages 242 to 252, are unchanged.

Within the type design section, a major change was made in the interest of reader convenience. In the Typophiles edition, a number of types not available at the time for letterpress reproduction were shown from printed proofs, segregated into unnumbered offset signatures at the end of each volume, with cross references to the main body of the text. These have now been inserted at the point where they are being discussed, even though this required deleting some folios and forced a sometimes uneven bottom page line. The specimens thus moved are Nos. 4, 8, 14, 18, 21, 23, 24, 28, 31A, 32A, 39, 41, 53, 54, 59, 63, 67, 68, 71A, 72, 76, 79, 85, 86, 111 and 114. No. 114 involved starting the Hebrew type account on Page 233 instead of 234. The Village Press mark was moved from Page 59 to 69.

As noted, the full alphabet of Goudy Thirty has been added on Page 229.

[*Colophon of the original edition*]

TYPOPHILE CHAP BOOKS XIII and XIV

A HALF-CENTURY OF TYPE DESIGN AND TYPOGRAPHY has been printed by Peter Beilenson, Mount Vernon, New York. Text composition, in Goudy Italian Old Style, by A. Colish, New York. Offset (not collotype as stated in the text): Meriden Gravure Company, Meriden, Conn. Photogravures: Photogravure and Color Co., New York. Of 825 copies printed 100 copies are reserved for contributors and so marked; 300 copies (numbered 1 to 300) are for subscribers, and 425 copies (numbered 301 to 725) are for general sale. This is Copy No. 401

Additional type for this second edition was set by Pat Taylor at the Suburban Letter Foundery, Larchmont, New York (named for Goudy's *Village* Letter Foundery, misspelled in this book by the editor's choice).